THE BRUCE OAK HEART

Tour of the King's Realm

Compiled by Jim Gilhooly

The Bruce Oak Heart
Compiled by Jim Gilhooly © 2024

For more information on the heart and its journey, feel free to contact us here
at the Robert the Bruce Heritage Centre, Renton, G82 4NB
or email us at: duncanthomson1960@yahoo.co.uk
meganrthomson@gmail.com
fifeview@gmail.com

Published by Robert the Bruce Heritage Centre, Renton
ISBN 978-1-0369-0765-5

In Commemoration Of The 750th Anniversary
Of The Birth Of Robert I, King of Scots.

The Bruce Oak Heart,
Tour Of The King's Realm.

A Tribute.
Born Turnberry Castle, Ayrshire
11th July, 1274.

Contents

1. Forward.

In this important book about Robert the Bruce yet again the Strathleven Artizans have succeeded in defining the character of the king in a way which reflects their commitment to uncovering the extraordinary story of his life.

Basing their research at 'Cardross' in the Vale of Leven where King Robert spent his last years, they have provided a unique perspective of his reign viewed from one of the few places in Scotland where he was able to live freely and in comfortable seclusion.

It was here, in this most precious place, that he chose to build a fine timbered and plastered Manor house to spend his retirement.

I commend this book as a fitting tribute to King Robert in his 750th anniversary year but also as the culmination of diligent and painstaking research.

Lord Charles Bruce, 12th Earl of Elgin.

2. Introduction.

*This publication primarily written to commemorate the **750th Anniversary of the Birth of Robert the Bruce** also describes the yearlong **Tour of the Bruce Oak Heart** around Scotland.*

*The story will describe the connection Bruce has to the modern day village of **Renton** in the **Vale of Leven,** the nearby town of **Dumbarton** and the **Loch Lomond** area where he spent his final years.*

*It will also tell the story of the centuries old '**Bruce Oak Tree'** which once stood in his estate in **Strathleven** and of the carving of reclaimed wood after the tree's demise, which was shaped into a **Symbolic Heart** and of the journey of this carved Heart to **Jerusalem** and the **Church of the Holy Sepulchre** in symbolic fulfilment of Bruce's final command to his faithful comrade the **Good Sir James Douglas** to take his heart there in atonement for the King's sins.*

*If you find yourself travelling from the Glasgow area on the way up North on the A82 to the Western Highlands then, after **Dumbarton** and before **Balloch** near the southern shore of Loch Lomond, make time to visit the **Robert the Bruce Heritage Centre** in the village of **Renton** – as it's manned voluntarily get in touch ahead of your trip and check for opening times.*

*Not only will you receive a warm welcome from these generous-hearted, dedicated folk, you will also get to see the **Bruce Oak Heart** and the replica **Royal Throne**, made from the salvaged wood from the **Bruce Oak Tree.***

*The Motto of the Bruce family is '**Fuimus'** meaning **'We have been'**, and with the continued efforts of such Historical Groups as the **Strathleven Artizans** who run the **King Robert the Bruce Heritage Centre** in Renton, then the King will continue to **'Always be'.***

Jim Gilhooly, Vale of Leven, 2024.

3. Commemorating the anniversary of the birth of Robert the Bruce.

The **11th of July 2024** is the 750th anniversary of the birth of a man known as **Robert the Bruce.** As **Earl of Carrick** he was to become **King Robert I** and renowned as the Warrior King who secured Scotland's independent sovereign status through a series of stunning military and political manoeuvres after suffering a number of crushing setbacks early in his Kingship.

This book is to commemorate not only the anniversary of his birth by highlighting his lifetime achievements - but also to praise the efforts made by many people from all different walks of life - both Scots and enthusiasts from overseas, who contribute to, and tirelessly promote, the history of Bruce and his Supporters in order to keep the memory of them alive - both in the present and for generations to come.

In addition to this, the story of Bruce and his connection to the **Bruce Oak Tree** which stood for centuries in the **Strathleven Estate**, land once owned by him while living out his final years before his passing on the 7th June, 1329, will also be told.

The modern day Strathleven Estate is located near the village of **Renton,** on the opposite side of the **River Leven** on the outskirts of **Dumbarton** in **West Dunbartonshire.** It's appropriate to tell Bruce's story and also that of the ancient tree connected to him which survived until relatively recently – and latterly 'brought back to life' through the work of local craftspeople who are part of a Historical Society in the area.

As far as a timeline is concerned the story that's going to be told here will take you back to the late **13th century** and up to the **present day.** Geographically we will travel from as far North as **St Duthac's Chapel** in **Tain** in the county of **Ross and Cromarty** and then we will make our way southwards throughout Scotland progressing onto mainland Europe to the town of **Teba** in the Andalusian region of southern Spain - and from there further eastwards to the 4th century **Church of the Holy Sepulchre,** in the Christian Quarter of the old **City of Jerusalem.**

This is a story 750 years in the making.

4. A tree of great antiquity, The Bruce Oak.

'The heart of the tree dies first'

The story about the tree's demise is a sad one. After standing for at least 700 years, (old enough for Bruce to have perhaps planted it), and with it possibly being up to 1,000 years old, the Bruce Oak was set fire to in an act of random vandalism in May 2004.

This ancient tree, if not planted by Bruce himself, could have been in existence during his lifetime and it is very conceivable for him to have passed by it, sheltered under it in rain, (or possible sunshine even), when walking or riding about his estate. We can but imagine.

The story of the tree's connection to Bruce could have eventually died along with its burning embers but thanks to a local Bruce Historical Society it was prevented from doing so.

Local people, proud of their area's connection to Bruce in his latter years as King, sought to have what remained of the tree salvaged from further attack and so, after lengthy negotiation, logistical planning and practical organisation, the remaining part of the trunk was taken away to be protected from further damage and decay.

The reclaimed parts of the tree were then 'repurposed' using local people's woodworking skills to fashion various medallions and ornaments for people to buy as keepsakes.

This would help them twofold, by promoting Bruce and his connection to the area to visitors and to invest the monies raised towards their Historical activities - with a strong emphasis on Youth / Community Organisation visits, Open Days & attendance at Fairs etc.

Approximate Location of the original site of The Bruce Oak near to Strathleven House.

5. A Brave Heart - rough hewn.

In the following years this Renton based historical group, **The Strathleven Artizans** (named to reflect the woodcraft element of their organisation), as part of their continued activities to raise awareness of Bruce's ties to the area, asked their Patron **Charles Bruce, Lord Elgin & Kincardine,** the head of the Bruce International Family, about the possibility of Bruce's Heart, buried in a casket in **Melrose Abbey** in the Borders, being taken to the **Church of the Holy Sepulchre in Jerusalem** to finally fulfil his wish for his Heart to be taken there in order to atone for his sins.

This pilgrimage was something Bruce was unable to do in person during his life as he had more pressing domestic matters to resolve.

Duncan Thomson, Chairman of the Artizans put this point to Lord Elgin and, although it was agreed that in theory this would be an incredible project, many people and organisations would need to be involved, and give authorisation for it to go ahead.

However, the planning, logistics - and not least the security of one of Scotland's greatest relics required to achieve this aim was deemed to be too complex to put into action and it was felt that it was best for Bruce's Heart to remain resting in peace in Melrose Abbey. Whatever your drive and ambition some decisions just have to be accepted.

Then one day **Arthur Murdoch** from the Artizans took a piece of the reclaimed Bruce Oak and decided to carve a representation of the King's Heart.

Once finished, this rough hewn symbol of Bruce's Heart, made from the ancient Strathleven Oak, then *'started to beat a new life of its own'.*

Here now is the tale of Robert the Bruce, King of Scots, The Bruce Oak, the Carved Heart from the ancient tree - and its journey to the Holy Land, Jerusalem and of the Heart's return to Scotland.

6. The birth and life of Robert the Bruce.

In the beginning; Bruce was one ten children, (and a half- brother to another), and the eldest son of **Robert de Brus, 6th Lord of Annandale,** and **Marjorie Countess of Carrick,** very much a mix of Scoto-Norman and Gaelic ancestry.

In addition to the **Lordship of Annandale,** the Bruces also held lands in **Aberdeenshire** and **Dundee,** and also substantial estates in **England:** Cumberland, Northumberland, County Durham, Yorkshire, Essex, Middlesex - and also **Country Antrim** in Ireland.

Bruce was born at **Turnberry Castle,** Ayrshire to a mother through whom he inherited the **Earldom of Carrick** and a father, (who, having been born in Writtle in Essex, is described as a 'Cross Border Lord), through whom he inherited the **Lordship of Annandale** and with that a royal lineage as a **Fourth Great-Grandson of David I** - giving him a claim to the Scottish throne.

After the death of **Alexander III,** (19th March 1286), **John Balliol** was selected by the Scottish auditors to be the King. However, there was dispute amongst the Scottish Lords, and **Edward I, King of England**, was asked to adjudicate. Seeing an opportunity to get involved in the affairs of Scotland he accepted and eventually **John Balliol** was proclaimed King of Scots.

It very much needs to be remembered that England and Scotland had lived alongside each other in 'relative peace' for many years prior to the **Wars of Independence.**

In those days, much as now, people moved throughout their lifetime - English to the North / Scots to the South, through marriage and inheritance - English born Parents having Scottish born children - and vice versa.

This of course led to sometimes complicated family politics – just think of loyalties being stretched and divided in Scottish households in later times such as the 17th& 18th century Jacobite Rebellions - and the 2014 Scottish Independence and 2016 Brexit Referendums as more recent examples.

Not everything in life is "black or white', and this also needs to be borne in mind when remembering Bruce, *(who was then a young man when Edward I started to lay his claim of Overlordship to the Scottish Crown),* deciding it best to be 'circumspect' and to initially protect his family & Estates from any retribution for 'non-compliance' of Edward's demands.

Edward was a seasoned warrior, a King of a country with well over 10 times the population of Scotland - and in command of one of the mightiest armies in Europe.

It was the Scots themselves who asked him to intervene in their own argument over who was to succeed after the death of Alexander III.

However hindsight is a great thing, the **Barons Letter**, (later to be known as the Declaration of Arbroath), of 1320 itself contains the statement:

"...that mighty prince the King of the English, Edward... when our kingdom had no head and our people harboured no malice or treachery and were then unused to wars or invasions, came in the guise of a friend and ally to harass them as an enemy..."

It's evident that in the beginning the Scots simply did not see what was to come after inviting Edward I to arbitrate in the decision making process of who the next Scottish Monarch should be.

When **King Alexander III** ruled Scotland his reign had seen a period of peace and economic stability and good relations with England.

On 19 March 1286, however, Alexander died after falling from his horse and the heir to the throne was Margaret**, Maid of Norway**, Alexander's granddaughter. As she was still a child, and in Norway, the Scottish Lords set up a government of Guardians.

Margaret fell ill on the voyage to Scotland and died in Orkney on the 26th of September 1290.

- ***Skelbo Castle** is a ruined 14th century keep, located near Dornoch in the county of Sutherland, located at a former ferry crossing and commanding views over Loch Fleet. It was here that Edward's commissioners were waiting for the arrival of the Maid of Norway where they learned of her death in Orkney in September 1290, aged 7 years, whilst on her voyage. Later in 1308, Bruce captured the Castle belonging to the **Sutherlands.***

The lack of a clear heir led to a period known as the **"Great Cause",** with several families laying claim to the throne. With Scotland threatening to descend into civil war, Edward I was invited by the Scottish nobility to arbitrate. Critically, before the process could begin, he insisted that all of the contenders recognise him as **Lord Paramount.**

In early November 1292, at a great feudal court held in the castle at **Berwick-upon-Tweed,** judgement was given in favour of **John Balliol** having the strongest claim in law. However Edward soon began getting involved in Scottish affairs and proceeded to reverse the rulings of the Scottish Lords.

He demanded homage to be paid towards himself, legal authority over the Scottish King in any disputes brought against him by his own subjects, contribution towards the costs for the defence of England, and military support was expected in his war against France.

Edward treated Scotland as a vassal state and repeatedly humiliated its new king.

The Scots soon grew disgruntled of their deeply compromised king; the direction of affairs was allegedly taken out of his hands by the leading men of the kingdom, who appointed a council of twelve—in practice, a new panel of Guardians—at Stirling in July 1295.

Under pressure from his council, Balliol not only refused support Edward militarily, but also formalised a mutual defence agreement with **Philip IV of France** against England, known in later years and to this day as the ***"Auld Alliance".***

Edward's response, on **30 March 1296**, was to sack the then Scottish Border town of **Berwick-upon-Tweed.** Capturing the town took just a few hours: killing many thousands of its inhabitants took several days.

The following month the Scottish army was subsequently defeated at the **Battle of Dunbar** in East Lothian on **27 April 1296.** By July of that year Edward was to force John to abdicate.

Edward instructed his officers to receive formal homage from some 1,800 Scottish nobles (many of the rest being prisoners of war at that time). **John Balliol** was seized by Edward's troops on 10 July, in the churchyard at **Stracathro** in Angus on Scotland's east coast.

Antony Bek, Bishop of Durham, representing Edward, forced John to renounce his alliance with the French King and made him sign a document admitting he had allied himself with his feudal overlord's enemies.

His surcoat was publicly stripped from his body, humiliatingly removing the arms of Scotland. Three days later, at Brechin, dressed in a plain white gown, John gave up his kingdom to Bek.

John was given the nickname of '***Toom Tabard'*** referring to the removal of heraldic insignia from his tunic as part of his submission. Balliol's ceremonial disrobing has been described as one of the saddest hours in Scottish history.

From now on, Edward I of England intended to rule Scotland directly, without the inconvenience of a Scottish King to complicate matters.

As a symbol of England's total domination he removed the **Stone of Destiny,** on which Scottish Kings had been crowned, from Scone to **Westminster Abbey**, where it was to remain until 15 November 1996, (apart from a brief and 'unofficial' journey north in early 1951).

Balliol was imprisoned in the **Tower of London**, however in 1299, deemed to be no longer a threat; he was allowed to return to his family estates at **Bailleu** in **France,** where he lived until his death in April 1313 at the age of 63. His claim to the throne passed to his son, **Edward Balliol.**

While these events of national importance were being carried out, back in 1295 Bruce was a young man of 21 years of age when he married **Isabella of Mar,** and on the 12th December 1296, their daughter **Marjorie** was born.

She would grow into young womanhood as the mother of the first Stewart, (Stuart), monarch of Scotland. However Isabella tragically died shortly after giving birth to Marjorie.

In **August 1296 at the age of 22, Bruce, as Earl of Carrick,** and his father **Robert, Lord of Annandale,** were among around 1,500 Scots at Berwick who swore an oath of fealty to Edward I of England.

Young Robert initially, would have wanted to have done right by his father who he himself would have judged it best to have kept on the right side of Edward – the memory of the vicious retribution that took place at the Massacre of Berwick – and the subsequent actions by Edward I. would have been fresh in young Bruce's mind.

However, in 1297 there was a growing rebellion against English rule, led in the south of Scotland by **William Wallace.**

When the Scottish uprising against Edward broke out in July **James Stewart, 5th High Steward of Scotland**, led into rebellion a group of Scots, including **Robert Wishart, Bishop of Glasgow** and **Macduff of Fife.**

Bruce had fallen under the influence of his **Grandfather's friends**, **James The High Steward** and **Bishop Wishart,** who had inspired him to take up with the resistance movement.

As Edward I was away in France at the time, he requested Bruce, and other Scottish Lords who had sworn fealty to him, to defeat the uprising.

Young Bruce left Carlisle and made his way to **Annandale,** where he called together the knights of his ancestral lands and, according to the English chronicler **Walter of Guisborough**, he addressed them thus:

No man holds his own flesh and blood in hatred and I am no exception.
I must join my own people and the nation in which I was born.
I ask that you please come with me and you will be my councillors and close comrades.

Despite **Wallace** and **Andrew Moray's** victory at **Stirling Bridge, 11th September 1297**, internal disputes amongst the Scots Nobility played a part in Wallace's defeat by the English at the **Battle of Falkirk, 22 July 1298.** After this defeat the young Bruce then again signed a treaty with the English, presumably with his fingers crossed behind his back, and he was able to keep his family lands.

However, Bruce was to accept the appointment of **Guardian of Scotland** in 1298 along with **John Comyn,** (who was in the pro- Balliol camp), and **William Lamberton, Bishop of St Andrews.**

Bruce eventually resigned from the position in 1300 due to his disagreements with **Comyn** and the possibility of John Balliol's restoration to the Scottish throne being a definite conflict of interest to the Bruce family's claim to the throne.

In 1302 Robert married his second wife, Irish noblewoman **Elizabeth de Burgh.**

On 22 April 1304, Edward I of England begins the siege of the strategically important **Stirling Castle,** held by **Sir William Oliphant** and 30 men.

The siege ended on 24 July after 3 months of bombardment by 12 siege engines including the infamous '**Warwolf'**.

Bruce, biding his time and needing to manoeuvre with incredible pragmatism against two powerful enemies, Edward I and the Balliol faction, was on the side of Edward at this time and was tasked with transporting the **Warwolf trebuchet** from **Inverkip** to the siege of Stirling Castle.

Bruce reported that the *'great engine of Inverkip'* was unmanageable and that no cart large enough could be found to carry it.

Letter from Edward I to Robert de Bruce, 16 April 1304.

This is the Edward's instruction for siege-engines to be fetched up to Stirling.

Translation:

"The king to the earl of Carrik, greetings.

We have well understood by your letters, which you send us by the bearer of the present, how you have arranged to cause our engines to be transported to Stirling; for which we are much obliged to you. And whereas you have informed us that you cannot find a waggon in the country able to carry the frame of the great engine which is with you, wherefore you wish that we should send someone to you who could find how the same frame could be conveyed by land; know that we will send some person to help you to do as soon as we well can do so.

But we charge you especially, that on no account do you desist from using all the pains and deliberation you can to cause the same frame to be carried to us, and stones, and all the other things appertaining to this engine, and to the other engines, as far as you can procure them. And for want of lead do not on any account desist from expediting the despatch of the said frame, and the timber, and the stones belonging to the said engine, and the others, together with all the lead which you can procure."

Bruce was clearly transporting a war engine of great size to the siege of Stirling. Edward had three large engines at the siege called **Belfry**, the **Parson** and **War-Wolf.**

The garrison were said to be most afraid, not of War-Wolf, but an engine *built 'higher than the castle walls'*. This is likely to be the description of **Belfry,** a massive siege tower.

The reference to the conveyance of stones in Edward's letter, 'appertaining to this engine', implies that the great engine conveyed by Bruce was a large trebuchet.

This could well have been War-Wolf. The letter might tally with **Pierre Langtoft**, who wrote that ***'Loup de Guerre'*** broke down on the way to Stirling and had to be fixed.

It seems Bruce repaired the monstrous contraption and had it sent on to the siege. It is fascinating to conjecture that Bruce was learning the skills and importance of castle assault and destruction while in the service of Edward I – skills he was later to utilise against the English and their Scots supporters.

There is no doubt about it that he was to apply his knowledge of English tactics against them – 'corralling' Edward II to encamp his army overnight hemmed in by the Bannockburn on three sides being one example .

In 1306, In **Greyfriars Church in Dumfries** Bruce had a meeting with **John Comyn** which soon escalated Bruce having accusing The Red Comyn of treachery and in the heat of the moment he mortally wounded Comyn leading to Bruce's papal excommunication.

Free of his Comyn rival, Robert faced a choice of ex-communication as an outlaw - or seize the opportunity and lay claim to the Scottish Throne. He decided to declare his Kingship and, with the backing of the Scottish church, he was declared King at **Scone Abbey** on **25 March 1306** in a ceremony conducted by **William Lamberton, Bishop of St Andrews.**
Isabella MacDuff, Countess of Buchan was a significant figure in the Wars of Scottish Independence. She was the daughter of **Donnchadh III, Earl of Fife**, and **Johanna de Clare**, daughter of The 6th Earl of Hertford. She married **John Comyn, 3rd Earl of Buchan**, and became **Countess of Buchan.**
John Comyn joined the English side after his relative was killed by Bruce - however Isabella did not share the views of her husband. According to tradition, the ceremony of crowning a Scots monarch was performed by a representative of **Clan MacDuff**, but Isabella, Lady Buchan, arrived in Scone the day after the coronation of Bruce.

However, Bruce agreed to be crowned for a second time as some would see the ceremony as being incomplete if not conducted by a MacDuff.
Responding to Bruce's crowning a furious Edward instructed his army commanded by **Aymer de Valence**, (who was to become the **Earl of Pembroke** the following year), to deal with Bruce and so Aymer based himself in **Perth**, (then St John's Town).

Bruce challenged him to come out from the castle's defences and to fight him in a pitched battle - but Aymer deemed it too late in the day for 'gentlemen' to fight so Bruce retired west to an area known as the **Den of Methven,** about 6 miles away.
However, in a surprisingly unchivalrous act by Aymer, (who actually had a reputation of being an honourable man), he attacked Bruce's camp overnight on the 19 June - while Bruce seems to have literally had his complete guard down.

It is possible that Edward's order to Aymer of ***"take no prisoners",*** signified by the carrying of a **red dragon flag**, had not reached Bruce's attention.
Bruce unhorsed Aymer in the first onslaught - but was unhorsed himself and nearly captured by **Sir Philip Mowbray -** only to be saved by **Sir Christopher Seton**.
Bruce was twice more unhorsed - and twice more rescued. At the last, a small force of Scots knights including **James Douglas, Neil Campbell, Edward Bruce, John of Strathbogie, Earl of Atholl, Gilbert de Haye** and the King himself formed a phalanx to break free, fleeing westwards.

This shattering defeat, left many of the king's most loyal followers dead, captured or soon to be executed. Those captured during the battle included **Alexander Fraser, David de Inchmartin, Hugh de Haye, John Somerville, Alexander Scrymgeour,** the royal standard bearer, **Thomas Randolph**, (Bruce's nephew), and **Hugh,** Bruce's chaplain.

West of Methven there is a place known as **Uamh-an-Righ,** (the King's Cave), above the northern shore of **Loch Voil,** and to add to the intrigue there is also a **Bruce's Stone** westwards of the cave on the northern shore of the Loch – there were to be many more caves attributed to Bruce during his flight westwards from Methven.
There is also a local tradition of Bruce being offered shelter at a place called **Cholliebhrochain**, (Wood of the Porridge / Brose), near **Blair Atholl**, in Perth & Kinross.
Not long after Methven the remnants of Bruce's routed force were again attacked, this time by the **MacDougalls**, (allies to the Comyns), at a place now known as **Dalrigh,** near Tyndrum in northern Stirlingshire. The name means ***"The King's Field"*** in Gaelic.

The MacDougalls had actually fought alongside **William Wallace**, but found themselves embroiled in the feud with Bruce due to their family ties with the Comyns.
According to folklore, Bruce found himself in a perilous rear guard action at Dalrigh as his army retreated. His horse was said to have been in a narrow space where it could not easily manoeuvre and as he became isolated a small group of MacDougalls almost pulled the king from his horse.

A MacDougall man is said to have attempted to pull Bruce from his horse by grabbing his cloak. Bruce killed him but lost his cloak in so doing. The dead MacDougall was found later still grasping the cloak with Bruce's brooch still attached. This brooch – or an altered version of it, is still in the possession of the clan to this day. The fact that Bruce even found himself confronted alone in this way alludes to a desperately serious situation, not only for Bruce and his immediate followers, but the entire cause of Scottish Independence. Despite being almost killed or captured, Bruce used his his skills at arms to fight his way through the attackers and join the remnants of his army in escaping.

There are two places that have prominence in relation to the folklore surrounding the battle.
Firstly, Bruce's men apparently threw their weapons into a loch during the retreat, (lightening their load and denying their enemies booty it is to be assumed), with the loch afterwards known as **Lochan nan Arm,** *(Loch of the Weapons / Swords).*

Secondly, the crossing point known as **Ath Chonachar,** *(Chonachar's Ford),* which is supposedly named after a piper in Bruce's army who was killed there after being struck by an arrow.
Bruce, and the remnants of his routed army, (possibly numbering up to 200 men), escaped south via the eastern shore **of Loch Lomond.**
In addition to the Bruce Oak that once stood in the Strathleven Estate there are a number of trees that have connections to Bruce.

- The **Bruce Yew** is located at a place called **'Stuc an t'Iobhairt'**, *(one translation is 'Place Of Shelter'),* near **Firkin Point**, (now a picnic spot), on the western shore of Loch Lomond.

- The tradition that Bruce read to his men on the banks of Loch Lomond originates in ***'The Bruce',*** composed by John Barbour, Archdeacon of Aberdeen, in the 1370s.

- Barbour in his epic poem claims that it was the story of **Fierabras** *('Ferembras' in Barbour's text),* a Muslim lord who converted to Christianity after being defeated in battle by Oliver, one of Charlemagne's Twelve Peers. The relevant passage is found at Bk. 3, ll. 435-66 in the original Scots.

Barbour tells how Bruce's small party came down to the eastern banks of Loch Lomond, (giving credence to either ***Rob Roy's Cave*** or the more southerly cave known as '***Rob Roy's Prison'*** found on this side of the loch being additional examples of the possible cave locations for the **'Legend Of The Spider').**

Bruce had the area scoured for means of transport over to the other side. **Sir James Douglas** is said to have found a small leaking rowing boat that would carry 2 men over at a time leaving the rower to return to pick up 2 more. Bruce, is said to have been the first man over along with Sir James.

With shelter and support offered by **Malcolm Earl of Lennox** when they reached the southern shore of Loch Lomond, Bruce and his party reached **Dumbarton** on the Clyde Coast where **Sir Neil Campbell** had organised shipping for them to sail westwards.

The northern English chronicles of **Lanercost** and **Guisborough,** state that Bruce was lurking either in the *'remote isles of Scotland'* or *'the furthermost isles of that country'*, both relating that Bruce utilised military support drawn from **Ireland and the Hebrides.**

Edward I seems only to have had intelligence that Bruce was *'hiding in the isles between Scotland and Ireland'.* Tradition has Bruce travelling to lands north of **Saddell,** located eight miles north of **Campbeltown** on the east coast of the **Mull of Kintyre**, to seek help from **Angus Og MacDonald**, *(Aonghus Óg Mac Domhnaill),* **Angus** as **Lord of Islay**, had taken Bruce's side due to his Clan's enmity with the **MacDougalls.**

Again, local tradition has Angus providing shelter, food and an escape plan as **Saddell Castle** is deemed too close to hostile clans who remain loyal to the rival Balliol and Comyn cause - including the nearby stronghold of **Castle Sween**, located on the eastern shore of Loch Sween in Knapdale.

Bruce and the remnants of his loyal following are then said to have been ushered to the safer fortress of **Dunaverty Castle**, on the most southerly point on Kintyre - and the closest point to Ireland, should an escape from Scotland be their required option.

According to **Barbour**, Bruce was harboured there for three days before Angus Og took him to **Rathlin Island,** off the coast of **County Antrim** as word had reached Angus that English ships were closing in to lay siege to Dunaverty Castle, and so Bruce was hastily taken aboard loyal **MacRuari** galleys to the safer reaches of Rathlin.

- As a result of supporting Bruce, and of he and his men's involvement in the Battle of **Bannockburn, Angus** received the **Lordship of Lochaber**, with **Duror** and **Glencoe**, as well as the islands of **Mull, Jura, Coll and Tiree.**

Barbour felt that Bruce had mostly remained hidden away on Rathlin, which is understandable as the Bruce family, from their main base in south-west Scotland, had naturally developed links with Ireland - as had their allies, the **Stewarts.**

The **Turnberry Band of 1286** had involved both Bruces and Stewarts in an agreement to support the **Earl of Ulste**r and **Thomas de Clare**.

The Earls of Carrick had long been involved in the affairs of Ireland and the Bruce Earls seem to have maintained that connection. The Carrick Earldom owned land on the Antrim coast and it seems likely Bruce would have used this strategic link when he needed to take refuge.

Allies of Bruce who were known to be actively supporting him perhaps give the best clues as to Bruce's whereabouts in the winter of 1306-7. Just like the Earls of Carrick, **James Stewart** also had land and a castle in Ireland on **Lough Foyle**.

The mention of an Irish ***'kinglet'*** in support of Bruce's two brothers, **Thomas and Alexander**, when they re-launched Bruce's military campaign in Galloway early in 1307 also suggests that Bruce was possibly present in Ireland while he was a fugitive.

The **Guisborough Chronicle** also refers to many Irishmen in his ranks on Bruce's return from the isles to Kintyre.

In addition to Dunaverty Castle, other refuge locations that Bruce might have escaped to include:

- **Dunyvaig Castle** on Islay, the **Seat of Angus Og**, (Bruce's first appearance in history is on the witness list of a charter that was issued by Alexander, (Alisdair), Og MacDonald, who was Lord of Islay before Angus.
- **Castle Tioram** on the shore of **Loch Moidart** on the Lochaber coastline, where he appears to have been offered support from ***Christina of Garmoran.**
- **__Garmoran__ is an area of western Scotland. It lies at the south-western edge of the present Highland Region. It includes __Knoydart, Morar, Moidart, Ardnamurchan__, and the __Small Isles.__*
- **__Christina__ was the daughter and sole heir of __Alan Macruarie, Lord of Garmoran__, and, therefore, had control over many areas in the west suitable for a fugitive: __Knoydart, Rum, Moidart, Eigg, Uist__ and __Barra__ among others.*
- *The medieval __Lordship of Garmoran__ was ruled by the __MacRuaris__ who were descendants of __Somerled,__ who later formed part of the __Lordship of the Isles__. __Castle Tioram__, at the entrance to Loch Moidart, being one of the residences of the lords of Garmoran).*
- According to the fourteenth-century **Gesta Annalia II,** Christina played an instrumental part in Bruce's survival, sheltering him along Scotland's western seaboard.
- **John of Fordun** refers specifically to Christina using her power and influence. Also known as **Christina of the Isles** she was married to Bruce's brother-in-law, **Duncan**, (he being the brother of Bruce's first wife, **Isabella of Mar**). There is, therefore, reason to suspect that Christina made a significant material contribution to the Bruce cause with funds, ships and men.
- **Eilean Donan Castle.**
    - The **Mackenzies** have a claim, (albeit unsubstantiated), in their clan history that Bruce was given shelter at **Eilean Donan Castle** – possibly just another example of those in positions of power looking to ingratiate themselves further with those who held ultimate authority. That said, it is on record that, in 1331, **Thomas Randolph, Earl of Moray,** sent an officer to Eilean Donan to warn the occupants of his forthcoming visit. In preparation 50 wrongdoers in the region were rounded up and executed, their heads being displayed on the castle walls - to Moray's approval.

- **Orkney.**

  - Orkney was under Norwegian rule at the time and could have been a possible destination – or **Shetland,** or even perhaps **Norway** itself where Robert's sister **Isabel Bruce** was queen dowager. *The suggestion that Norway and/or the Orkneys and Shetlands were possible refuges is probably based on the fact that Bruce's wife and daughter were heading in the direction of Orkney after escaping from* ***Kildrummy Castle*** *just before Aymer de Valence captured it. Bruce's sister,* ***Isabel,*** *had married into the Norwegian royal family and by this time was the widow of the late King Eric and sister-in-law to King Hacon. Isabel was an influential lady and could help provide refuge for her brother either in the Orkneys, or in Norway itself.*

The Legend of the Spider.

The legend's first appearance was thought to have been in **Sir Walter Scott's *'Tales of a Grandfather'.*** However it seems to have appeared 200 years earlier in a **History of the Douglas family** by **Hume of Godscroft.**

In it, it was **The Good Sir James Douglas,** Bruce's close friend and ally, who saw the spider and made mention of it. According to the book, Douglas told the tale to Bruce while he was a fugitive in the Hebrides.

Douglas likens Bruce's losses in battle by the winter of 1306-7 to the efforts of a spider climbing a tree with his web and failing twelve times.
The spider climbed the tree on his thirteenth attempt and Douglas encouraged Bruce to follow the spider's example and try and regain his kingdom.

These were desperate times for Bruce and his men, the Chronicler **John of Fordun** relates that, in derision of Bruce's hopeless and unknown condition, a sort of ribald proclamation was made after him through the churches of Scotland, as *'lost, stolen, or strayed'.*

Left: King's Cave, Drumadoon.

Right: Kingscross, Arran, where Bruce departed for the mainland, Holy Isle in the background.

The Return of the King.

Wherever Bruce did end up staying we do know that he would return to mainland Scotland the following year from the **Isle of Arran** in early 1307 to continue his campaign to regain control of Scotland.

John of Fordun reports that Bruce *'after endless toils, smart, and distress, got back, by a round-about way, to the earldom of Carrick'.*

The start of his campaign began by splitting his forces in two and, while he returned to Carrick landing near the the earldom's chief castle at **Turnberry**, his two brothers, **Alexander and Thomas**, landed in **Loch Ryan** in **Galloway** where they were opposed by the **Macdowells.**

The Bruce brothers were defeated and they were both captured and executed. In the meantime, landing on his home soil of Ayrshire, Bruce would create the momentum for a highly successful campaign which included the use of a wide range of military and political strategies.

These included lightening 'commando like' assaults and withdrawals; employing subterfuge and guerrilla tactics - all to avoid pitched battle. Also threats and bribery techniques were applied to avoid bloodshed, and truces agreed in order to buy time to better prepare for inevitable conflict.

These tactics were a mix of either combined, or individual involvement between Bruce and his main Commanders – notably the **Good Sir James Douglas** and **Thomas Randolph Earl of Moray** his nephew:

List of notable events prior to the Battle of Bannockburn:

Spring of 1307 - Turnberry Castle, Ayrshire.

Ahead of his arrival back on the Scottish mainland Robert had had sent agents to Carrick late 1306 to collect his Martinmas rents. His attack on the English garrisoned in Bruce's own family Castle was only partially successful. However it ultimately led to the withdrawal of the English soldiers. He ordered the destruction of the castle later in 1310 to prevent it from falling once again into their hands. The ruins that remain are part of the original castle as it does not appear to have ever been rebuilt.

March 1307 - Moss of Raploch, Galloway Forest Park.

- Bruce was hiding from English forces in the surrounding hills when he discovered the presence of a small English force bivouacked ususpectingly on 'Moss Raploch'. Seeing their guard was down he attacked them.
- His small Scots force picked over the dead bodies looking for weapons and booty. By no means a major engagement, this was still a victory and the news spread. The actual site of the battle is now covered by the reservoir of **Clatteringshaws.**

April 1307 - Glentrool.

- The English were commanded by **Aymer de Valence**, this was another minor engagement, but an important one, spreading the message of another of Bruce's victories. Glen Trool is a narrow glen in the Southern Uplands of Galloway. Loch Trool is aligned on an east–west axis and is flanked on both sides by steep rising hills, making it ideal for Bruce's ambush.

10th May 1307 - Battle of Loudon Hill.

- The English were again commanded by **Aymer de Valence**. It took place beneath Loudoun Hill, in Ayrshire and the battle was deemed to be Bruce's first 'recognised' military engagement.

7th July 1307 - Edward I's death- and succession of his son Edward, Prince of Wales.

- Bruce had put into action his ambitions first against his Scottish rivals, the **Balliol / Comyn / MacDougall alliance** before dealing with Edward II.

- Edward II had promised an expedition to Scotland in 1308 and encouraged his Scottish based supporters to take a truce offered by Bruce until August when he hoped to lead an expedition into Scotland.
- However, as contemporary English chroniclers report, the great court rivalry among the English nobility took priority with him.
- Edward II also seemed to be waiting for the 'right moment' to strike back in Scotland, the end result was a delayed English response which gave Bruce time to consolidate his support and further weaken the resolve of his Scots opponents.

The attack and capture of Castles that were garrisoned by Bruce's English and Scots enemies include:

Oct / Nov 1307:

1. **Inverlochy Castle,** by modern day Fort William, Lochaber.

Nov 1307 > 1308:

2. **Urquhart Castle**, Loch Ness, Inverness-shire.
3. **Inverness Castle.**
4. **Tarradale Castle,** East of Muir of Ord / Western end of the Black Isle.
5. ***Skelbo Castle,** Dornoch, Sutherland.
    - *It was at **Skelbo** in 1290 that the Scottish Commissioners were staying overnight, on their way north to meet the Maid of Norway, when news came of her death. They stayed two nights in Skelbo, in consultation with the English Commissioners, and then rode on to Wick, presumably to obtain proof of her death on board ship near Orkney.
    - The castle was burned down by Bruce when the Moravia Sutherland family supported England in the Wars of Scottish Independence. The keep and curtain wall was rebuilt in stone.
    - William, second Earl of Sutherland attended in 1283-84 the Parliament which accepted the Infant Margaret of Norway as Queen of Scotland he also supported Bruce's claim to the throne and at Berwick in 1296 signed the homage roll - but later adhered to Edward I.
    - William, son of William and third Earl of Sutherland. A minor when his father died, succeeded in 1306-7. His ward was given to John, younger son of the Earl of Ross. In 1308-9 the young Earl attended Parliament at St Andrews. Sir Robert Gordon states that the Earl fought at Bannock burn 1314 which gave Bruce the rule of Scotland. The Earl signed in 1320 the letter of the nobles to Pope John XXII known as the Declaration of Arbroath asserting full independence of Scotland from the English Crown.
6. **Nairn Castle.**
7. **Elgin Castle.**
    - The castle was eventually sacked and slighted after 2 previously unsuccessful attacks during Bruce's harrying of Buchan. The castle was repaired by Thomas Randolph, (d.1332), who was granted the earldom of Moray by his uncle, Bruce in the period 1312-14.
8. **Banff Castle**
    - Bruce became sick during the seige of **Banff Castle** probably owing to hardships of a lengthy campaign. While recovering and leaving **John Comyn, the 3rd Earl of Buchan** unsubdued at his rear.

Further battles and capture of castles include:

Christmas / New Year 1307 / 1308 - **Skirmish at Slioch.**

- After falling seriously ill at the seige of Banff Bruce retreated to a more secure position at **Slioch**, just east of Huntly. His enemies, the **Earls of Buchan** and **Atholl**, made an unsuccessful attack on Christmas Day. A second attempt on 31 December found Bruce's position too strong, and he was able to withdraw to safety - and prepare for the decisive victory at **Inverurie / Battle of Barra.**

23 May 1308 – **Battle of Inverurie, *(aka Battle of Barra)* – and the subsequent defeat of the English Garrison in Aberdeen, July 1308.**

- Robert finally achieved his landmark defeat of Comyn at the Battle of Inverurie. He then overran Buchan and defeated the English garrison at **Aberdeen Castle.** The harrying of Buchan was ordered by Bruce to make sure all Comyn family support was extinguished. Lack of English support contributed to the capitulation of the north to Bruce.

Aug 1308 – **Battle of the Pass of Brander / Ben Cruachan & the taking of Dunstaffnage Castle.**

- The only major northern force not under Bruce's military control by mid-August 1308 was that of the **Macdougalls.** The MacDougall's had made a truce with Bruce as he proceeded north to Inverlochy in 1307.
- That truce must have ended by August when Bruce was also free from other distractions in the north to concentrate his efforts on Argyll. **John MacDougall of Lorn**, (John the Lame), had been ill through the winter of 1307-8 and remained at **Dunstaffnage Castle.**
- In March 1308 he wrote a letter to Edward II complaining of the threat from Bruce's large army and the lack of support from their barons, and asking for English aid. Bruce ordered more 'harryings' in **Argyll** and **Kintyre** in the territories of Clan MacDougall. With these acts, Bruce successfully destroyed the power of the Comyns who had controlled most of Northern and Southwestern Scotland for over one-hundred and fifty years.
- Bruce then crossed into Argyll and defeated the MacDougalls, allies of the Comyns, at the **Battle of the Pass of Brander** subsequently seizing **Dunstaffnage Castle.**
- After the battle Bruce held what is considered to be the last Scottish Parliament ever conducted in Gaelic at **Ardchattan Priory** close to the north shore of Loch Etive, five miles inland from its mouth near the modern day **Connel Bridge**

Bruce's campaign in the north was matched by his Brother Edward's campaign in Galloway. It was a bloody campaign as reported by the **Lanercost Chronicle:**

- *'Meanwhile, taking advantage of the dispute between the King of England and the barons,* ***Edward de Brus****, brother of the oft-mentioned Robert and* ***Alexander de Lindsey*** *and* ***Robert Boyd*** *and* ***James de Douglas****, knights, with their following which they had from the outer isles of Scotland, invaded the people of Galloway, disregarding the tribute which they took from them, and in one day slew many gentry of Galloway, and made nearly all that district subject to them.'*

Despite **Barbour's** claim that Bruce succeeded in taking thirteen castles in Galloway, this overstates Bruce's control in the south and south-west, where most of the well-fortified castles such as **Caerlaverock, Dalswinton, Bothwell, Lochmaben, Loch Doon and Dirleton** were in English or pro-Comyn hands - as well as Royal Castles such as **Wigtown, Lanark, Dumfries** and **Ayr**.

- During **March of 1309, Robert held his first Parliament at St. Andrews.**
- By **August of 1309** he would control all of Scotland North of the River Tay.
- **On 23rd February 1310** the **Declaration of the Clergy and People** was issued in favour of Robert the Bruce by the Church of the Friary Minor in Dundee.
- The Declaration gave support to Bruce's campaign against the English and was issued to proclaim Bruce's kingship to the General Church Council, which was gathered in France. The Declaration was a prelude to the better-known **Declaration of Arbroath of 1320**, in which Scotland declared her independence and the right to defend herself against attack.

- Feb 1312 - **Dundee under siege – surrendered in April.** Edward Bruce captured the castle held by Constable **William de Montfichet**. Dundee Castle was strategically very important protecting the trading port.

- Spring of 1312 – **Perth.** In the previous year of 1311, Bruce and his followers besieged the town of Perth but were unable to breach the defences. In the following year another attempt was made:

"Bruce would not desist from his purpose, or suffer this single walled town for ever to baffle his efforts. Providing himself with scaling ladders, and such other instruments that he could find, he speedily renewed the siege, at a time when those within the town were pleasing themselves with the persuasion that they were enclosed within impregnable walls and had no future siege to fear.
He chose a dark night and, in its silence taking a chosen band, conducted them himself in person, partly wading, partly swimming across a ditch deep broad and full of water that surrounded the walls. The rest were animated on this, as on many other occasions, by the example of the daring valour with which the King exposed himself the foremost to danger.

The contest among them was who should first cross the ditch, and, by the scaling ladders which they had carried with them, mount the walls. This gallant and perilous enterprise succeeded. The King himself was second to enter the town. The garrison and townspeople were easily overpowered.
In the castle, and in the stores of the merchants, a considerable booty was found of those things which the captors wanted the most for the relief of their own necessities.
The slaughter of the vanquished was humanely stayed as soon as the resistance ceased. The houses were burned and the walls and fortifications levelled with the ground. By this happy achievement all Perthshire and Strathearn was freed from servitude to the English and reduced under the authority of King Robert."

- **August 1312 - Invasion of Northern England:** Hexham, Corbridge and Durham.

- **September 1313 - Linlithgow Castle captured by Bruce's followers**.

    - **Edward I made Linlithgow his base** during his campaigns of 1296 and 1301, and expanded it in 1302-3. The site remained in English hands and, in 1310; Edward II spent a week at Linlithgow during one of his Scottish campaigns.

    - With the first royal manor existing on the site in the 12th century it ever since has been in nearly constant use. It was replaced by the English with a fortification known as ***'the Peel'.***

    - The fort was retaken by an ordinary Scot in 1313. **John Barbour's poem 'The Bruce'** describes at length how a cattleman named **William Binning of Bunnock,** who usually sold hay to the garrison of the peel, stopped his wagon at the gate so that it couldn't be closed. Following this blockade, eight of his companions hidden under the hay, jumped out of the wagon, Binning is said to have slain the porter with a single blow and captured the peel for Bruce, who then sent reinforcements and dismantled the fortification.

- **21st June 1313 -** As well as raiding into the Northern part of England, Bruce landed at **Ramsey** in the **Isle of Man** and laid siege to **Castle Rushen** in **Castletown**, capturing it would deny the island's strategic importance to the English.

- **19th Feb 1314 - Roxburgh Castle taken.**

    - Assault led by **Sir James Douglas.** James Douglas's strategy in capturing the fortress of Roxburgh was one of his most brilliant schemes. Douglas took the **Roxburgh Castle** in 1314, alongside a few of his men. Wearing cloaks and disguised under cowhide, they made their way to the castle. Mistaking Douglas's army for cattle, the English-men fell for their trap.
    - In the dark of the night, Douglas's men crept up to the castle. Using a rope ladder, they climbed up. The defenders, overwhelmed by such a sudden ambush, failed to protect the fortress, a thus it fell into the hands of James Douglas and his men. The castle was then slighted so that the Englishmen would not be able to use it again.

- **14th March 1314 - Edinburgh Castle taken.**

    - Assault led by Bruce's nephew, **Thomas Randolph, Earl of Moray.** Edinburgh Castle sits atop the formidable Castle Rock, looming over the city below for centuries. Its strategic position has made it a coveted fortress and victim of sieges throughout Scottish history, despite being notoriously difficult to capture. On the 14th March 1314, Thomas Randolph, Earl of Moray, set out to do just that in a daring night attack.
    - Edinburgh Castle was impregnable. Its position on Castle Rock set its summit at 430ft above sea level, with the rocky cliffs on its south, west, and north sides at 260ft high. Leaving only the main gate on its east as the key access point and with a heavy English guard inside, Randolph faced quite the challenge. He enlisted the help of **William Francis**, the son of the former governor of the castle, who used to climb down a hidden path on the rock face to visit his secret lover in the city below.
    - On the night of the 14th March, Francis led Randolph and around thirty of his men up the unforgiving rock face. In darkness and in silence, this must have been harrowing – one false move and they would tumble to their deaths, and one noise and they would alert the English guards above of their arrival.
    - While Randolph's small group scaled the cliff, another body of his troops attacked the main gate of the castle to distract the garrison. When they finally reached the top of the cliffs, Randolph and his men rushed over those previously unassailable walls and fought the garrison inside, working their way to the front of the castle to raise the gate for the rest of Randolph's forces. After successfully taking the castle, it was burned to the ground to prevent it from falling into English hands again, sparing only the chapel of St Margaret
    - This was a triumphant success for Randolph, levelling the playing field between himself and Douglas, as well as ramping up the pressure on Edward II. Only three months later, Randolph would play a crucial role in the Scots' victory at the Battle of Bannockburn over Edward's forces, delivering Stirling Castle into Scottish hands. After seven years of turning around the defeats of Methven and Dal-righ – and a deliberate refusal to meet with the English in pitched battle on even ground, had caused many to consider Robert as one of the great military leaders of any age.

- **25th May 1314 - The siege of Stirling Castle.**

    - On or about this day in 1314 Edward Bruce Earl of Carrick and King Robert's younger brother, made a deal with **Sir Philip Mowbray**, commander of the garrison for the relief of Stirling Castle. Though not necessarily sanctioned by King Robert himself, this deal would prove to be the pivotal moment that led Bruce to give battle after Edward II headed his army into Scotland in order to relieve it.

23 / 24 June 1314, The Battle of Bannockburn.

Left: Bruce Oak Heart. Photo courtesy of Duncan Thomson, Chairman of the Strathleven Artizans.

Right: Bruce Oak Pike Spearhead Medallion.

These listed military achievements culminated in Bruce deciding in meeting the army of Edward II in pitched battle. His tactics resulting in the defeat of the English and the recognition of his military genius.

6 April 1320 - Declaration of Arbroath.

- Due to continued harassment by Edward II, in 1320, Scottish nobles and churchmen signed the **Barons Letter,** latterly known as the Declaration of Arbroath, declaring Robert as the rightful king of Scotland.
- Dated 6 April 1320 and addressed to **Pope John XXII** it constituted King Robert I's response to his excommunication for disobeying the pope's demand in 1317 for a truce in the First War of Scottish Independence. The letter asserted the antiquity of the independence of the Kingdom of Scotland, denouncing English attempts to subjugate it.
- Generally believed to have been written in **Arbroath Abbey** by **Bernard of Kilwinning (or of Linton**), then **Chancellor of Scotland and Abbot of Arbroath**, and sealed by fifty-one magnates and nobles, the letter is the sole survivor of three created at the time.
- The others were a letter from Bruce himself and a letter from four Scottish bishops all of which made similar points. The Declaration was intended to assert Scotland's status as an independent, sovereign state and defend Scotland's right to use military action when unjustly attacked.
- The pope later agreed and recognised Bruce as King.
- The **'Tyninghame'** copy of the Declaration from 1320 is kept in the **National Archives of Scotland**
- After Edward II was deposed as king in 1327, the English made peace with Scotland.

17 March 1328 - Treaty of Edinburgh-Northampton.

The treaty was signed in Edinburgh by Bruce and was ratified by the Parliament of England meeting in Northampton on 1 May.

Signed by Edward III of England recognising Scotland as an independent kingdom.

The terms of the treaty stipulated that in exchange for £20,000 sterling, the English Crown would recognise:

- The Kingdom of Scotland as fully independent;
- Robert the Bruce, and his heirs and successors, as the rightful rulers of Scotland.
- The border between Scotland and England as that recognised under the reign of **Alexander III** (1249–1286).
- One of two copies of the document, which was written in French, is held by the National Archives of Scotland in Edinburgh.
- However, the document does not constitute the entire peace treaty, which was contained in a number of indentures, notarial instruments and letters patent issued by Edward III and Robert I. Since none of them survives, not all details of the peace treaty are known.

7. Death of the Warrior King – the Heart goes on crusade.

Although this publication has been intended as a summary of Bruce's life in the 750th anniversary year of his birth it is highly appropriate to also cover his death and give a bit more detail on the actions of one of his leading Commanders, the **Good Sir James Douglas,** in fulfilment of the King's final wishes.

Bruce died on the **7th June 1329** just short of his 55th birthday at the ***'Manor of Cardross',*** on the banks of the **River Leven** in the modern day area of **Dalquhurn,** part of the village of **Renton,** near to the town of **Dumbarton.**

Before dying, Bruce requested that his heart be taken to the Holy Land. He prayed to many Saints during the course of his life and it would not be far fetched to think that he may have had the killing of **The Red Comyn** in consecrated ground in Greyfriars Kirk and the **Hership, (Harrying), of Buchan** to gain complete control of his Comyn rivals power base at the forefront of his mind when praying for forgiveness so that his soul may enter the gates of heaven.

He commanded that, after his death, Sir James Douglas should take his embalmed heart and bear it with him on crusade, thus fulfilling the pledge that Bruce had been unable to honour in his lifetime.

The chronicler **Jean le Bel** tells that Bruce wanted his heart taken to the Holy Land and presented at the Church of the Holy Sepulchre whereas the poet **John Barbour** says merely that Bruce wished his heart to be carried in battle against 'God's foes.'

"I will that as soone as I am trespassed out of this worlde that ye take my harte owte of my body, and embawme it, and take of my treasoure as ye shall thynke sufficient for that enterprise, both for your selfe and suche company as ye wyll take with you, and present my hart to the holy Sepulchre where as our Lorde laye, seyng my body can nat come there"

In the **spring of 1330**, armed with a safe conduct from **Edward III of England** and a letter of recommendation to **King Alfonso XI of Castile**, Douglas set off from **Berwick** and sailed first to **Sluys** in Flanders.

Here, according to the contemporary chronicler **Jean Le Bel,** Douglas' company consisted of one knight banneret, (it's not clear whether this 'knight banneret' was Sir James himself), six ordinary knights and twenty esquires.

Other knights named by John Barbour included **Sir William de Keith**, ***Sir William de St. Clair of Rosslyn** and the brothers **Sir Robert Logan** and **Sir Walter Logan**.

Others alleged at one time or another to have accompanied Douglas are ***John de St. Clair**, (younger brother of Sir William), **Sir Simon Lockhart of Lee**, **Sir Kenneth Moir**, **William Borthwick**, **Sir Alan Cathcart** and **Sir Robert de Glen**.

From **Berwick**, Jean le Bel relates that the Scots party sailed to Sluys a port located in the west of Zeelandic Flanders, in the south-western Dutch province of Zeeland.

Douglas is described as 'holding court' on board ship for 12 days as if the late king were present.

Le Bel states that Sir James' main purpose was to publicise his mission and find out if other knights were interested in joining the Scots expedition to the Holy Land.

It may be the case that Sir James was awaiting news of the planned crusade against **Granada** and on learning that King Alfonso still intended to go to war, despite the withdrawal of his allies, Sir James finally set sail for Spain.

After a stormy passage the party arrived at the mouth of the **Guadalquivir,** sometime in late June, and disembarked upstream at **Seville.**

According to Barbour, Douglas presented his credentials to Alfonso XI, no doubt aware of Douglas's reputation throughout Christendom, Alfonso offered him riches, armour and horses.

Douglas politely declined these gifts, declaring that he and his men were prepared to offer their arms in the service of the king as humble pilgrims, seeking absolution for their sins.

Alfonso accepted and assigned experienced soldiers, accustomed to the style of fighting on the *'Frontera'*, as advisors to Douglas and his fellow knights.

While the Scots rested after their long voyage and waited for the expedition to depart, many foreign knights who had come to seek service with Alfonso paid their respects to Douglas, including a number of Englishmen who were keen to meet the man who had once been their enemy.

At the formation of Alfonso's army Barbour claims that Douglas was given command of the lead division, the *'vaward'* or vanguard however it might have been the case that he was put in charge of all the foreign knights in the Castilian army.

This Christian Host marched to **Ecija** then to **Osuna** on the frontier. Once across the border, Alfonso continued south to the meadows of **Almargen,** five miles west of **Teba,** from where he advanced to set up camp and assault the fortress.

While Alfonso waited for his siege engines to come up from **Ecija,** a Muslim Granadan relief force was forming in **Malaga.**

This was under the command of **Uthman ibn Abi al-Ula**, a Berber noble fighting in the service of the sultans of Granada, who set off with six thousand cavalry and an unknown number of infantry to the relief of Teba.

Marching up the **Guadalhorce valley**, Uthman's force crossed over into the valley of the river **Turón** where they pitched camp between **Ardales castle** and the supporting **fortress of Turón**, ten miles south of Teba.

The Christian Host was hampered by limited access to water and it was necessary on a daily basis to drive their livestock out of camp and down to **Río Guadalteba**, the river flowing two miles south of the castle.

Uthman quickly identified this vulnerability and sent raiding parties to disrupt the watering details. Alfonso in turn sent out patrols to hold them off and there were frequent skirmishes between the two sides. It is possible that Sir James Douglas was killed in one of these encounters.

The chronicle, ***'Gran Cronica de Alfonso XI',*** refers to a confrontation on the river that resulted in the death of ***"a foreign count... through his own error",*** although some commentators think Douglas died in a more decisive encounter some days later.

Alfonso's problems included the imminent departure of five hundred Portuguese knights who had declared that their term of service was about to expire.

Meanwhile, siege engines arrived at Teba and operations began to open a breach in the walls of the castle. One night the Muslim garrison of Teba sallied out to attack the siege lines and retired leaving a siege tower in flames.

Uthman had concluded he could not defeat the Christians in open battle and so devised a stratagem to force Alfonso to abandon the siege.

Under cover of darkness, three thousand Moorish cavalry prepared to make a diversionary attack across the river while Uthman took another three thousand upstream to make a flank attack on Alfonso's camp. At dawn, Uthman's river contingent occupied the watering grounds of the **Guadalteba.**

Alfonso, however, having been warned by his scouts of the enemy's movements, kept the main force of his army in camp while he sent **Don Pedro Fernández de Castro** with troops to check the assault developing on the river.

Some argue that Douglas and his contingent must have been part of this reinforcement.

With battle joined, **Uthman** believed that his ruse was working and, emerging from the valley where he and his men had been concealed, rode up to attack the Christian camp from the west.

When he reached the col, *(the lowest point of a ridge or 'saddle' between two peaks),* overlooking the **Almargen valley** he saw the camp bristling with Alfonso's men armed and ready while at the same time saw his men on the river downstream beginning to fall back. He instantly abandoned the attack and rode back to support his right wing but arrived only in time to join in the general retreat.

The Moors on the river had been unable - or reluctant, to resist the Christian counter-attack.

When Alfonso, having seen Uthman withdraw, sent **Rodrigo Álvarez de las Asturias** with a further 2,000 men to intervene, the Moor Granadan retreat turned into a rout.

Barbour, in his description of Douglas' last battle, describes a similar rout, with Douglas and his contingent pursuing the fleeing enemy closely.

There is, however, no mention of the **Siege of Teba** in Barbour's account, which describes the Christian army advancing from **Seville** to repel an invasion from **Morocco.**

According to Barbour, Douglas outruns the rest of his men and finds himself far out in front with only ten or so followers. He turns back to rejoin the main body too late, the highly mobile Moorish cavalry see their opportunity, rally, and counter-attack.

In the running fight that follows, Douglas sees **Sir William St.Clair** surrounded by a body of Moors, trying to fight his way free.

With the few knights still with him, Douglas rides to the rescue but all are killed, including **Sir William St.Clair** and the brothers **Sir Robert** and **Sir Walter Logan.**

The Castilian sources do not mention any Moorish counter-attacks during the pursuit, despite the Moors' notorious capacity for turning on unwary pursuers.

The Castilian forces pursued the Moorish army back to their camp in the **Turon valley**.
The chance of a more comprehensive victory was lost when the Christians stopped to loot the enemy tents and baggage.

Despite further skirmishes, **Uthman** made no further attempt to raise the siege and shortly afterwards the garrison of Teba surrendered. The aged Berber general died some weeks later.

Barbour tells how Douglas' body, together with the casket containing the embalmed heart of Bruce, were recovered after the battle and carried back to Scotland by Sir William Keith of Galston, who had not taken part in the fighting because of a broken arm.

Bruce's heart was laid to rest at the **Abbey of Melrose**, Bruce held great affection for the Abbey and had left instructions that his heart was to be interred there, while his body was to be buried at **Dunfermline Abbey**, the traditional last resting place of Scottish kings.

Douglas' body was interred at **St Bride's** chapel, at Douglas, Lanarkshire. Thereafter the Douglas coat of arms displayed a **crowned heart** in remembrance.

Most of Robert's tomb was destroyed during the Scottish Reformation, but on 17th February 1818, workmen employed to build a new parish church on the site of the eastern choir of Dunfermline Abbey discovered a tomb before the site of the high altar of the former abbey.

8. Teba Festival – commemoration of The Good Sir James.

The Village of Teba celebrate James Douglas and his comrades involvement in the siege of Teba with an annual festival.

The festivities include the traditional historical re-enactment through the streets of Teba and in the **Estrella castle**, guided tours, a medieval market with music and a medieval encampment, and also Arabic and Celtic music, a Moorish and Scottish tapas route and workshops in pottery, coin minting and glass blowing, amongst others.

There are numerous cultural associations who collaborate with the organisation of the Douglas Days event including: the Saint Andrew´s Society of Gibraltar, the Alzar el Vuelo cultural association, the Hisn Atiba association, the Order of the Knights Templar of St Michael and the Scottish Cultural Association: ***The Strathleven Artizans.***

Left: Monument to Sir James Douglas, Teba.

Right: Effigy of Sir James Douglas carried aloft, pics courtesy of Cha Halliday.

Douglas Days Festival attended by the Strathleven Artizans.

9. The Strathleven Artizans – in the valley of the King.

"King Robert the Bruce Lived In Renton From 1326 – 1329. Where You Now Stand A King Once Stood."

The Strathleven Artisans are based on the Old Ticket Office, Renton Train Station, near Dumbarton.

They are a not-for profit Historical Society run by volunteers who describe themselves as being intent on promoting the life and times of King Robert the Bruce and his connection to the Strathleven area where he spent the remaining years of his life.

Robert the Bruce, died in his 'Manor House of Cardross' in the modern day village of Renton on the banks of the River Leven on the 7th June 1329 and the Strathleven Artizans aim to educate as many people as possible not only in Scotland, but all around the world on his life achievements.

In their free to visit / voluntarily run Heritage Centre - and reflecting the 'Artizan' description in the group's title, there is a replica of Robert the Bruce's Throne, suits of armour, original paintings, artefacts and medieval weapons - and even a small library filled with books about Scottish History that you can flick through during your visit.

The village of Renton is near the ancient Capital of Strathclyde, Dumbarton, on the historical site of the King's manor house and they describe their soul aim as to inform of the 'Royal Connection' and rich medieval history 'soaked in the surrounding areas'.

In spreading the word of Scotland's greatest King, they visit schools all over the country, sharing their knowledge with a 'hands-on' approach to learning.

Descendants of Robert the Bruce attended the official opening of the centre on Saturday, 27 March, 2010.

Lord and Lady Elgin, along with their son Lord Bruce, were guests of honour at the event on to mark the transformation of the former Renton train station into a facility to celebrate the life of the Bruce.

The centre, launched on the anniversary of Bruce being crowned King of Scots in March 1306.

The Artizans, who dressed as lords and ladies of Bruce's time, kicked off the celebrations with a march from Renton's Tontine Park along to the station where they were greeted by Lord Elgin, who is patron of the group. Lord Elgin's grandson performed the honour of officially opening the centre.

Duncan Thomson, Chairman of the Artizans, said:

"Our hope is that the centre will attract tourists on their way to Balloch to get off the train at Renton and get information on Robert the Bruce living and dying at Renton.

The centre has been transformed inside and out, with displays, art and information on Bruce, his manor house and his life at *Pailleanflath, in Renton.

****Pailleanflath**, a Gaelic word which means both **Tent of the King** and **Pavilion of the Great Hero.***

There are also artefacts, donated by historian Stuart Smith, collected from the area including pieces of pottery and jewellery which have been dated to around the time the king of Scots would have roamed his estate.

The ceiling has been adorned with artworks created and donated by artist Duncan Brown depicting four generals who fought alongside Bruce against King Edward II of England in the famous 1314 battle.

Artizans member Paul Hunter has created visionary paintings depicting his dreams of Bruce including a piece showing the hero's manor house.

The group now has the patronage of Andrew Bruce, Earl of Elgin and Kincardine, chief of the international Bruce family.

10. Selection of online articles regarding Robert the Bruce's connection to the Renton area.

A), Harry McAllister spreads the word in US

TUESDAY, 25 MAY 2010

Bowman Harry McAllister sends us a copy of information he recently sent to The Highlander magazine in the United States:

I wanted to pass on some information about a development of historical consequence which has taken place in Scotland.

On Saturday, 27 March, 2010 the King Robert Bruce Heritage Centre was opened in Renton, Dunbartonshire, a small Town next door to my Hometown of Dumbarton.

The official opening was performed by Lord Elgin, a direct descendent of Robert and the senior Bruce today.

Robert Bruce lived the latter part of his life in the Dumbarton area, and died there in 1329. But, somewhat incredibly, the location of his Manor House became lost.

Both Dumbarton and Renton were heavily industrialized in the 19th Century and the first half of the 20th and the terrain in the area where the House may have been situated had been built on and roads and railways had run through it.

In 1996 a group of Dumbarton men, including myself, formed the 'Bruce Committee' to see if we could pin-point the location of the Manor House.

After doing considerable research on the subject we brought in Prof. Geoffrey Barrow, whose 1960s (?) book on Bruce is credited with being the most detailed and accurate rendition of Bruce's life.

I remember us walking the banks of the River Leven (which drains Loch Lomond into the River Clyde), looking at the topography of the land, studying old maps and letting Prof. Barrow give his opinions on possible locations.

We eventually settled on a Farmer's field as our best guess and we engaged the Department of Archaeology at Glasgow University (which, to my surprise, was run at that time by an American) to conduct 'geophysical surveys' of the area

To cut a long story short, nothing of significance was discovered. Traces of manmade structures were found, but the ground had been so disturbed over the centuries that it was not possible to draw any real conclusions.

The project was eventually abandoned and the Bruce Committee disbanded. Fortunately, the Committee's work had drawn attention to the Bruce mystery and others became interested. The Strathleven Artizans, a group which had formed in Renton, decided to continue the hunt for Bruce's house.

The thought was that if a Bruce connection could be established, a missing piece of Scottish history would be brought to light and the now economically devastated town would benefit from visitors both from within Scotland and outside. Two things have happened that have aided 'the hunt.

First, the operators of the railway which passes though Renton allowed the Artizans to 'adopt' the now unused railway station and this has become, with a great deal of effort, the King Robert Bruce Heritage Centre (KRBHC). Then, land clearing being done in Renton for new housing, uncovered some plaster that, I believe, has been identified as medieval or at least very old.
Whether this is from the Manor House or some other structure has not yet been established, but the possibilities have the Artizans, and others, very excited. Several things stand out to me in this story. An important missing piece of Scottish history could be resolved; Renton could receive not only some financial gain, which it can certainly use, but a lift to its self-esteem (particularly for youngsters) which it needs relative to what must be seen as a very uncertain future.
It is also a marvellous example of what a small group, starting basically with nothing, can accomplish. Diane and I know the Artizans well, we have met with them many times during our visits to Scotland and we are extremely impressed with what they have done.
I know first-hand that Lord Elgin, a man born into the upper class and who lived his long life in such circles, thinks the world of the Artizans - a group of working class men, and a few women, many of whom have no work today and have had none for a long time. This story says a lot about these people and it says a lot about Lord Elgin.
I do not know nearly enough about King Robert Bruce, but I do know a few things. The most important of these is that he was a popular King when the Declaration of Arbroath was written (1320) in which the people state they will gladly give their life to Bruce but they also state that if he does not follow the People's wishes he will removed from the throne and 'another man' will be given the job.
What the people did at that time was to establish that it was they who were the true 'Sovereign', I think it was the first time in human history that occurred.
Diane and I have the utmost respect for the Strathleven Artizans. They do a great deal with very little. We wish them the very best.
Harry McAlister.

B), Robert the Bruce's Manor House.

Despite a report that appeared in The Observer on Sunday 22 February 2009 stating that the buried ruins of the manor house of Robert the Bruce had been found in the Pillanflatt area of Renton, this interpretation has yet to be confirmed.

While there is strong Charter evidence to indicate the presence of a manor or hunting lodge belonging to Bruce in the area, this is more likely to have been located in the vicinity of Mains of Cardross, to the south of the Pillanflat, rather than in the area to the north of it.

Stone, plaster and mortar are not generally susceptible to scientific dating techniques, and lime mortar was used from the Roman period up to the late 19th or early 20th centuries.

According to Bruce Historian **Stuart Smith**, a charter dating from 1362 charter states that **Robert the Bruce resided between Kings Park of Cardross and the lands of Pillanflatt, bounding the lands of Dalquhurn.**

This would suggest a site to the south of the Pillanflat, but to the north of Castle Park, in the vicinity of what is now Mains of Cardross.

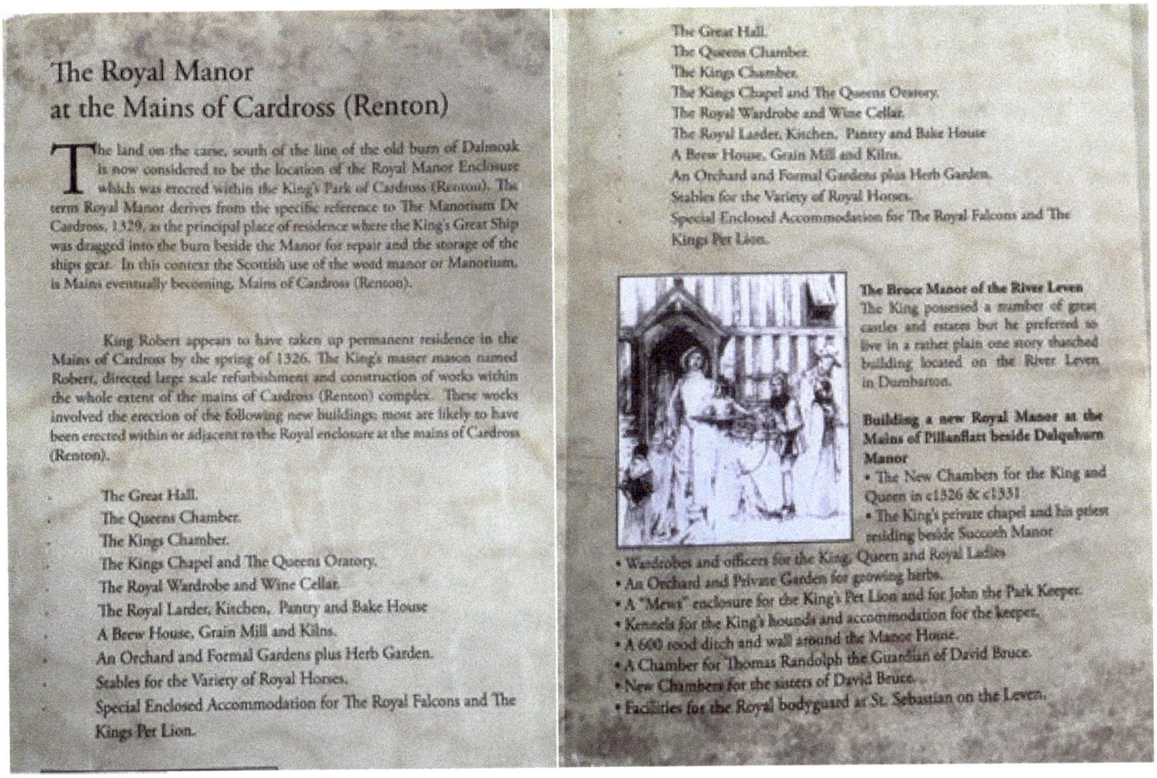

The Royal Manor at the Mains of Cardross (Renton)

The land on the carse, south of the line of the old burn of Dalmoak is now considered to be the location of the Royal Manor Enclosure which was erected within the King's Park of Cardross (Renton). The term Royal Manor derives from the specific reference to The Manorium De Cardross, 1329, as the principal place of residence where the King's Great Ship was dragged into the burn beside the Manor for repair and the storage of the ships gear. In this context the Scottish use of the word manor or Manorium, is Mains eventually becoming, Mains of Cardross (Renton).

King Robert appears to have taken up permanent residence in the Mains of Cardross by the spring of 1326. The King's master mason named Robert, directed large scale refurbishment and construction of works within the whole extent of the mains of Cardross (Renton) complex. These works involved the erection of the following new buildings; most are likely to have been erected within or adjacent to the Royal enclosure at the mains of Cardross (Renton).

- The Great Hall.
- The Queens Chamber.
- The Kings Chamber.
- The Kings Chapel and The Queens Oratory.
- The Royal Wardrobe and Wine Cellar.
- The Royal Larder, Kitchen, Pantry and Bake House
- A Brew House, Grain Mill and Kilns.
- An Orchard and Formal Gardens plus Herb Garden.
- Stables for the Variety of Royal Horses.
- Special Enclosed Accommodation for The Royal Falcons and The Kings Pet Lion.

The Great Hall.
The Queens Chamber.
The Kings Chamber.
The Kings Chapel and The Queens Oratory.
The Royal Wardrobe and Wine Cellar.
The Royal Larder, Kitchen, Pantry and Bake House
A Brew House, Grain Mill and Kilns.
An Orchard and Formal Gardens plus Herb Garden.
Stables for the Variety of Royal Horses.
Special Enclosed Accommodation for The Royal Falcons and The Kings Pet Lion.

The Bruce Manor of the River Leven
The King possessed a number of great castles and estates but he preferred to live in a rather plain one story thatched building located on the River Leven in Dumbarton.

Building a new Royal Manor at the Mains of Pillanflatt beside Dalquhurn Manor

- The New Chambers for the King and Queen in c1326 & c1331
- The King's private chapel and his priest residing beside Succoth Manor
- Wardrobes and officers for the King, Queen and Royal Ladies
- An Orchard and Private Garden for growing herbs.
- A "Mews" enclosure for the King's Pet Lion and for John the Park Keeper.
- Kennels for the King's hounds and accommodation for the keeper.
- A 600 rood ditch and wall around the Manor House.
- A Chamber for Thomas Randolph the Guardian of David Bruce.
- New Chambers for the sisters of David Bruce.
- Facilities for the Royal bodyguard at St. Sebastian on the Leven.

C), Let the Bruce Rule the Rock: Strathleven Artizans dedicated to King of Scots.

Daily Record, 21 FEB 2019.

As we launch our campaign this week, we spoke to history group **Strathleven Artizans** who have spent over a decade sharing their love of Robert the Bruce with the World.

The Strathleven Artizans have spent 15 years tirelessly travelling the globe sharing the tales of the great Scottish king's life in West Dunbartonshire.

The passionate group work all year round to spread the word across the country and further as to how big a role this region played in the history of the King of Scots.

Their Robert the Bruce Heritage Centre in Renton is filled to the brim with fascinating artefacts and information detailing the life and times of the outlaw king.

One of their many prized pieces is a wooden throne, carved from the Bruce Oak tree which fell in 2004.

The great oak, which was believed to be more than 700 years old, is thought to have been planted as a young tree around the same time Robert the Bruce lived on the land near to the, (modern day), Strathleven House (by) Dumbarton.

The group's website has also inspired keen history enthusiasts to join up from countries all over the globe and they spend their time visiting schools and appearing at events all over Scotland to share their knowledge.
Chairman Duncan Thomson told the Lennox Herald:

"Our website gets almost 3000 hits a day and we have people all over Europe and as far as New Zealand who are Artizans. We do this for Robert the Bruce. We feel like we work for him and all we want to do is share this history with as many people as possible. "We have travelled to 10 different countries all over the world to tell the stories of Robert the Bruce's connection to West Dunbartonshire. This place is absolutely hoaching with history. It is fascinating and it's right on our doorstep."

In August last year, some members of the Artizan's travelled to **Teba in Spain** to take part in the **Douglas Day festiva**l, which celebrates the exploits of Sir James Douglas.

The festival commemorates the adventures of the Scottish knight, who was tasked with taking the **embalmed heart of King Robert the Bruce** to the **Holy Sepulchre in Jerusalem.**

The Spanish town features a **Sir James Douglas Museum** as well as a **plaque dedicated to both James Douglas and King Robert the Bruce.**

The Strathleven Artizans have been attending this event for over 10 years alongside thousands of other history enthusiasts.

Artizans member **Brian McCutcheon,** who portrays Robert the Bruce, feels something should have been done in West Dunbartonshire long ago to commemorate the King of Scots. He said:

"This is a fantastic event held in Spain which celebrates a Scottish hero. I just don't understand why we don't do anything like that here, especially in this area which has so much history to offer.
"We are in danger of losing this history if more is not done to make it known to as many people as possible. "If it is not taught then it will be gone."

The group — which boasts 30 dedicated members — are well known in the community, particularly among historians, for their passionate efforts, with the leader of the Bruce Clan**, Lord Elgin**, regularly keeping in contact with the group.

Lord Elgin, who attended at Dumbarton in 2001 for the unveiling of the plaque at St Serf's Church in Levengrove Park to honour the church as a burial site — also presented members with special **carved oak hearts from the famous Bruce Oak tree.**

Duncan added:
"It means a lot to us that he recognises the work that we do. He knows we do it for the love of Robert the Bruce and the history and I think that is why he likes to keep in touch with us.
"He knows that passing on this history means just as much to us as it does to him and that is a big honour for us."

The group are right behind the **Lennox Herald's Let The Bruce Rule The Rock campaign** and say they would love to see something official done to mark the significance of the King of Scots in the area.

Duncan said:
"We think this is a fantastic idea. We would love to see the people of this area come together and have this history officially recognised. "It should have been done long before now. It's such a waste.
"I would love to see a monument similar to the stag at Lomondgate near to Pailleanflath of Bruce holding his sword. That would be amazing."

Fellow member Nicky 'Heilan-Spirit' added:
"There are so many places in the town that people could see. And having more to let people know how much history there is around the town might encourage people to stay in the town and spend more time here which can only be a good thing."

She added that the group have already seen an increase in visitors since the release of **blockbuster Netflix movie Outlaw King,** which tells the story of the legendary Scottish hero while on the run.

Duncan and other members of the Artizans made a special trip to **Dunfermline Abbey** for a screening of the movie and **presented director David McKenzie with a Great Seal of Robert the Bruce and a Bruce Oak Heart.**

Duncan added:

"We are seeing a surge of people visiting our centre since the film's release. It's been fantastic.
"I don't think as a town we are doing enough to make the most of it. We should be investing millions into this as it deserves to be celebrated and made known to everyone."

D), The Bowmen of Saint Sebastian and the Strathleven Artizans.

Sebastian is among those remarkable martyrs, brave men and women of faith, who have been canonized (declared a saint), by the Roman Catholic Church.

Today he is venerated as the patron of soldiers and athletes, including **archers.**

An officer of the Roman Praetorian Guard during the rule of Emperors Maximian and Diocletian, he was also a "secret Christian", something which had it become known would have identified him as a "marked man".

During the time of his military service he was able to protect the lives of many Christians who would otherwise have been martyred. Inevitably, his Christian sympathies become known and his arrest and execution ordered.

He was tied to a post set into the ground and used as a target by archers.

Assumed dead, he was cut down and his body given into the keeping of a woman named Irene. Miraculously, she discovered that he was still alive, and though he was gravely injured, no arrow had done lethal damage.

She nursed him back to health, and he was sufficiently recovered at a later date to publicly confront the emperor concerning the persecution of Christians.

Once again he was ordered executed [288 AD], this time successfully. Irene was also canonized.

According to tradition, during the later years of the reign of King Robert I, "THE BRUCE" a group of forty soldiers were recruited and trained as the king's personal bodyguard and designated the "Forty Bowmen of Saint Sebastian".

These were notable men who took responsibility for the safety of the king, and service to his name and family. They pledged their allegiance to the king and his family with their very lives.

Today, the "**THE FORTY BOWMEN OF SAINT SEBASTIAN"** has been revived in Scotland under the auspices of another group known as the "Strathleven Artizans", (officially as the "King of Scots Robert the Bruce Society") who are pledged to the service of The Name And Family Of Bruce and to the legacy of King Robert I.

Sir Andrew Bruce, Earl of Elgin and Kincardine, Knight of the Thistle, and 37th hereditary chief of the Name and Family of Bruce, is the patron of this organization.

The Artizans achievements are many, including the **construction of a replica of King Robert's throne.**

The Bowmen are a select few individuals who through long and notable service to the Name and Family of Bruce, and in anticipation of future service, have been honored in ceremony and gifted with a very unique mark of that honor.

Rather than an elaborate and bejeweled medallion, the Bowmen wear a simple cut wooden heart hung around the neck with a leather thong.

Not long ago, a huge **old oak tree in Strathleven,** on property once owned by King Robert, and which according to tradition was just a sapling during his lifetime, caught fire, the damage terminal.

The Artizans preserved all of the salvageable wood from this tree and have executed a number of works of art, including parts of the replica throne, using this wood.

The heart worn by today's Bowmen is of this wood.

It is a great honor for each of them to wear this heart over their own. It is reminiscent of the knights who pledged to carry the heart of King Robert on crusade to the Holy Land, at his own request, and as his death became imminent.

Today's Bowmen are pledged to emulate the life and legacy of King Robert, and to serve, protect, and proclaim the Name and Family of Bruce.

William P. Bruce – February, 2017

E), The Bruce Oak – its death and resurrection.

The Bruce Oak was a tree that stood in the grounds of Strathleven House, West Dunbartonshire. This estate was owned by Robert the Bruce and by the early 21st century, the tree's trunk was 8.8 metres (29 ft) in girth and reached 5.5 metres (18 ft) in height.

It was thought to have been between 700 and 1,000 years old and was one of the oldest oaks in Scotland. The tree was subject to an arson attack in May 2004, when a fire was lit within its trunk, and it fell the same month.

A local history society, the Strathleven Artizans, originally made the connection between the tree and Robert the Bruce and took custody of its timber. The trunk was cut up, and members of the society claimed to be able to see the face of the Bruce in its cross section.

A petrified acorn was also found in the timber. The society planned to carve a heart out of the oak to take to the Church of the Holy Sepulchre in Jerusalem.

It was one of the Bruce's last requests that his heart be taken there by his champion James Douglas, Lord of Douglas, as he had not been able to fulfil his wish go on a crusade to the Holy Land. However, whilst carrying the heart, Douglas was killed in battle against the Moors at the Battle of Teba in 1330.

The Strathleven Artizans also used some of the timber from the oak to construct a replica of Robert Bruce's throne. The inspiration came from a depiction of Bruce sitting on a throne on his royal seal. The carving was carried out by **John Donaldson** and an expert from Historic Scotland, taking eight years to complete.

The throne also incorporates yew from a tree at Elderslie, the birthplace of William Wallace – another Scottish patriot, and ancient olive wood from Teba. The throne has four beast heads at the ends of the arms and clawed feet.

The throne was unveiled at Dunfermline Abbey by Andrew Bruce, 11th Earl of Elgin.

It was later displayed at the Battle of Bannockburn visitor's centre at the ***Bannockburn Live*** event of 28–29 June 2014 to mark the 700th anniversary of the Bruce's victory.

Using an image from the Bruce's official cast metal seal, which he used to authenticate documents, the group set about building a recreation of a throne the King sat on during his 23-year reign.

The seal shows the Bruce sitting on a throne with clawed feet and the carved heads of four beasts, supposedly to protect him from attackers from all sides.

'Captivating tale'

As well as wood from the Strathleven tree, the wooden support for the throne is made from yew timber from Elderslie, the birthplace of William Wallace.
Ancient olive wood from Teba Spain is also incorporated to mark Robert the Bruce's embalmed heart being carried into battle by Crusaders there in 1330.
Duncan Thomson, chairman of Strathleven Artizans, said the story of Robert the Bruce had "captivated people for generations".
He said: "We hope that in tirelessly reconstructing his throne to commemorate the 700th anniversary of the Battle of Bannockburn, we once again bring the great monarch's story to life, not only to those who are familiar to it already but to a whole new audience and for future generations.

"This project has been both a celebration of traditional skills and a tool for education for both young and old."

'Talking point'

Along with a number of other backers, including renowned wood carver John Donaldson, Historic Scotland got involved in the project by providing the skills of a master carpenter using traditional techniques.
Conservation director David Mitchell said he was "very pleased" Historic Scotland could help with the project.

He said: "While minimal evidence made it difficult to recreate a wholly authentic throne, the process of re-creating it and highlighting aspects of Bruce's life are just as important in this case, and it will certainly be a talking point.

"Incorporating wood from sites across the country and further afield, the throne is a celebration of traditional skills and helps to tell Bruce's story."
The replica throne is being unveiled at Dunfermline Abbey by the Earl of Elgin, a descendant of the Bruce and backer of the project, before it is taken to the Bannockburn Visitor Centre for the two-day Bannockburn Live event over the weekend.

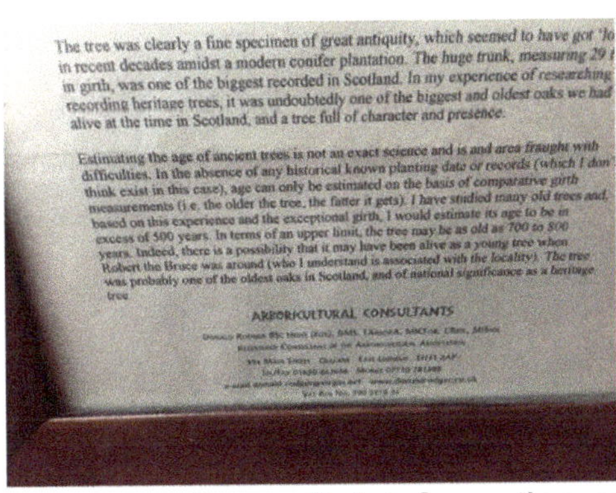

The tree was clearly a fine specimen of great antiquity, which seemed to have got 'lo in recent decades amidst a modern conifer plantation. The huge trunk, measuring 29 in girth, was one of the biggest recorded in Scotland. In my experience of researching recording heritage trees, it was undoubtedly one of the biggest and oldest oaks we had alive at the time in Scotland, and a tree full of character and presence.

Estimating the age of ancient trees is not an exact science and is and area fraught with difficulties. In the absence of any historical known planting date or records (which I don' think exist in this case), age can only be estimated on the basis of comparative girth measurements (i.e. the older the tree, the fatter it gets). I have studied many old trees and, based on this experience and the exceptional girth, I would estimate its age to be in excess of 500 years. In terms of an upper limit, the tree may be as old as 700 to 800 years. Indeed, there is a possibility that it may have been alive as a young tree when Robert the Bruce was around (who I understand is associated with the locality). The tree was probably one of the oldest oaks in Scotland, and of national significance as a heritage tree.

ARBORICULTURAL CONSULTANTS

Bruce Oak information and Carved Heart Medallion

Renton Heritage Centre Workshop & Bruce Oak Crafts.

Elements of the Bruce Oak were also incorporated into a replica of Bruce's throne, based on his Royal Seal.

THE GREAT THRONE

King Robert the Bruce's Great Throne

The History of the Bruce Oak.

The Bruce Oak, also known as the Strathleven Oak was at one point the oldest and largest Oak tree in Europe. It was planted 700 years ago and it is believed to be planted by King Robert himself or that he built his sons Manor House at Strathleven under the Oak Tree.

Enter the Artizans

In December 2006 the Artizans were made aware of the tree and we took possession of it. We waited 8 long years for the Oak to naturally dry out and be usable. We agreed that with this wood we would produce a National Exhibit and display. This would be known as The Great Throne.

The Finished Product

The Artizans partnered with Historic Scotland to make the Throne. We added 9 other historic, prominent pieces of wood to the Throne that connect to a part of Bruce's story. These woods are:

1. Bruce Oak.
2. Scone Oak
3. Bannockburn Oak
4. Teba Olive Wood
5. Jerusalem Olive Wood
6. Culross Abbey Laburnum
7. Broom Hall Oak
8. Ballendrick Oak
9. Dalmoak Oak
10. Wallace Yew.

For more information on the Throne visit:
www.strathlevenartizans.com
or visit our Facebook Page:
King of Scots Robert the Bruce Great Hall and
Or call 07783739453

Painting on display at Renton Heritage Centre by Artist David Severeide.
A symbolic scene depicting Bruce as a young man contesting in a joust.

Left: **'The Pavilion of the Great Champion'** and Bruce's Sleuth Hound, **Donachd**, *(Duncan).*
Right: In the distance **Dumbarton Rock** and the **River Clyde.**

Bruce's War Horse **Nesbit.** He named it after the Nesbits who were Hereditary Horse Breeders.

F), The Bruce Oak Heart, a symbolic representation of the Heart Of Bruce finally taken to the Church of the Holy Sepulchre, Jerusalem to fulfil the King's final wish.

"This is probably the most amazing post that we have ever put up. Carrying out King Robert the Bruce's last wish. We the people, the community of the realm pray for the soul of our greatest king, Robert the Bruce. ***Duncan Thomson, chairman of the Robert the Bruce Heritage Centre, 24 June 2022.***

G), Palestinian orphan fostered in Renton takes effigy of Robert the Bruce's heart to Jerusalem. *Daily Record 13 JUL 2022:*

Duncan Thomson, chairman of the Robert the Bruce Heritage Centre, wanted to honour the King of Scotland's dying wish, which was for his heart to be taken to the Holy Land to be forgiven.

A Palestinian orphan who was adopted by a Renton family over 30 years ago took a wooden heart in memory of Robert the Bruce 3,500 miles to Jerusalem to honour the King's dying wish.

Simon Collings from Palestine was brought up in Renton and is an ambassador for the Robert the Bruce Heritage Centre in the town.
The centre's mission is to educate and promote Robert the Bruce's importance to Renton, where he lived his final three years and died.

Duncan Thomson, chairman of the Robert the Bruce Heritage Centre, wanted to honour the King of Scotland's dying wish, which was for his heart to be taken to the Holy Land to be forgiven.

He said: *"When he died in Renton, his last wish was for his heart to be taken to the holy land to ask God for forgiveness for all the people he had killed to free Scotland. And that was never fulfilled.*
"We own the Strathleven Oak, which was planted by him, on the grounds of his palatial manor house in Strathleven.
"One of our carvers made a heart out of the Bruce oak in our interpretation of Robert the Bruce's heart.
"We made the decision to take it to Jerusalem to fulfil his wish.
"A young man, Simon Collings, from Palestine who was adopted by a Renton family over 30 years ago took the heart to the Holy Land whilst out visiting family in Palestine.
"I asked Simon if he could take the heart to the slab, kiss it and say prayers for Robert the Bruce for all the people he killed and ask for forgiveness.
"He did, and it was on the June 24, the anniversary of the battle of Bannockburn. It was amazing."
The reason Robert the Bruce's heart never made it to the Holy land was because Sir James Douglas, who was taking the heart, was killed in Spain. His heart was then returned to the borders of Scotland.
Duncan spoke to the Lennox and said he got quite emotional knowing they had carried out Bravehearts' dying wish, saying: "It was a massive favour.

"Honestly, the buzz about the place when we released our social media post of what had happened was crazy. Over 21,000 people had read the post which is 10 times as much engagement as we usually get on social media.
"If you remember, Carman Hill went on fire a couple of months ago. My friend Jim had done a post, with a photograph of the fire that night, which said that it signified the King's heart being restored and put to rest. "I started greeting, to be honest."

H) Strathleven Artizans – Chairman's Message.

On 7th June a 54 year old man lay on his death bed at his home in Renton. He was weeks away from his 55th birthday. He was a tremendously successful man. He was loyal and kind. He was surrounded by his family, his bishops and his most loyal friends. He had one final wish. The last thing he would ask of his loyal friend. And the last thing he would say before passing away in his sleep.

'Take my heart to the church of the most holy sepulchre in Jerusalem and ask God for forgiveness.' He then died and the streets were said to be filled with wailing when the people heard that their hero was no longer alive.

The man was King Robert the Bruce and the man he asked was Sir James 'the good' Douglas. His right hand man and the only one he could trust to carry out this most important task. It was one last request from a king to his warrior and friend.

So in the beginning of the next year James Douglas and a group of knights leave Scotland to begin the journey to the Holy Land to grant their King's final wish.

Sir James arrives in Spain in August of 1330 and finds the country in turmoil. A war is on-going between the Spanish and the Saracen army.

King Alfonso the Great hears about these brave, fierce knights and their mission and asks them to join his army and help them. At first, the Black Douglas refuses but after much persuasion eventually agrees to help King Alfonso and in doing so is struck down and killed in the Battle of Teba alongside 10 other brave Scottish knights.

This is devastating in two ways. First obviously, being the death of James Douglas who was one of the most skilled knights Scotland had ever known. And the second being that the King's heart was never taken to the Holy Land. Instead it was taken back and buried in Melrose Abby in the borders of Scotland.

King Robert the Bruce's last wish was never fulfilled. Until today.

Today, on the anniversary of the Battle of Bannockburn and 692 years after he died, our ambassador ***Simon Collings*** *took two items that were made from a 700 year old Oak tree that was planted by the King in the grounds of his palatial manor house in Strathleven to the holy place in Jerusalem.*

One being a heart shaped necklace and the other being a replica of the king's heart. He lay them down and said a prayer over them hereby fulfilling the final wish of a man who was on his deathbed.

When both hearts return to Scotland members of the 40 bowmen of St Sebastian will have a ceremony and bury them here in his home country, his most beloved Scotland.

So after hundreds of years King Robert the Bruce's final wish was granted.
On the anniversary where Scotland's greatest king gave the Scottish people their independence making him their hero. And subsequently placing him in the hearts of the Scottish people forever.

Simon Collings taking the Bruce Oak Heart from Renton to the **Church of the Holy Sepulchre in Jerusalem**, a symbolic gesture in fulfilment of Bruce's final wish.

The **Church of the Holy Sepulchre** in the **Old City of Jerusalem** stands on a site that encompasses both **Golgotha, (or Calvary)**, where Jesus was crucified, and the **tomb (sepulchre)** where he was buried.

Also known as **The Church of the Resurrection**, this site has been an important pilgrimage destination since the 4th century, and it remains the holiest Christian site in the world.

This limestone slab, about six meters long and one meter wide, commemorates the anointing and preparation of Jesus' body for burial.

A moor fire on the **Carman Hill** overlooking the Vale Of Leven around the time of the Bruce Oak Heart returning to Scotland – reminiscent of a cortege of mounted knights carrying torches aloft – perhaps a sign of the return of the King's Symbolic Heart from the Holy Land?

Display Panel, Robert the Bruce Heritage Centre.

The body of Sir James Douglas carried aloft by Moors in his honour.

11. The Bruce Oak Heart: Tour of the King's Realm, a pictorial guide.

Preparation for taking the Bruce Oak Heart on a pilgrimage throughout Scotland.

Left: Something to read on the journey.

Right: Strathleven Artizan,*'Urban Highlander"* models Sir James Douglas attire while holding the Bruce Oak Heart.

Left: Sgian Dhu, with replica Bruce Coin in its handle.

Right: The Bruce replica Throne - both Sgian & Throne fashioned from the Bruce Oak.

Travel Casket containing the Bruce Oak Heart.

Cushioning to protect the Heart on the journey.

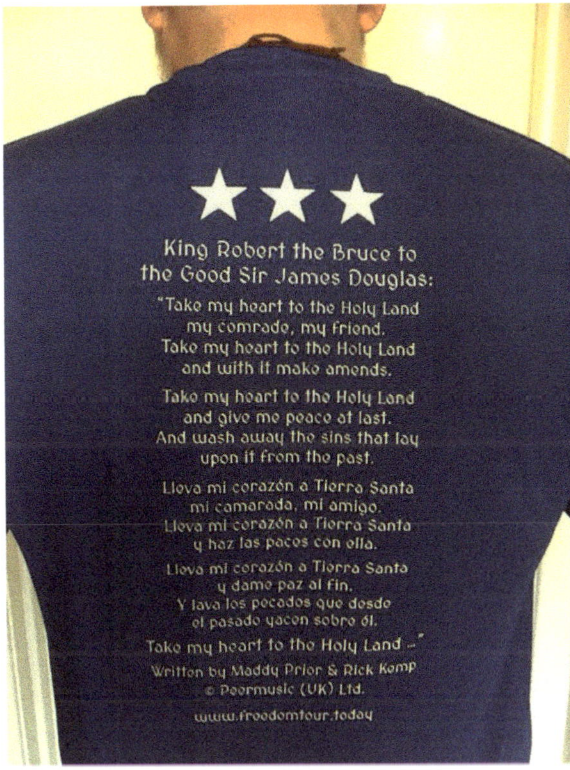

Left: James Douglas attire, courtesy of
Stephen Hughes of **Scottish Superheroes T-Shirts & Hoodies.**

Right: Bruce Oak Medallions from the **Robert the Bruce Heritage Centre, Renton.**

Left: Castle Hill, Dumbarton – King Robert's Weather Vane points the way.

Right: Old plaque on Weather Vane pole by Dumbarton Patriotic Association:

"In commemoration of

King Robert the Bruce who resided at Castlehill adjoining

and died there 7th June 1329."

(NB: The location of Bruce's Manor now identified as nearer to the River Leven by Renton).

Setting off, St Serf's Chapel, Levengrove Park, Dumbarton.

St Serf's, location for the internment of Bruce's viscera ahead of his burial in Dunfermline Abbey

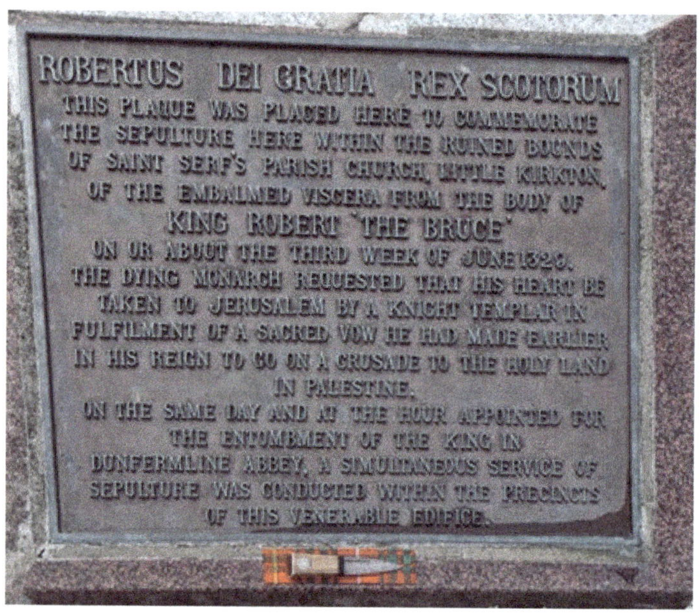

ROBERTUS DEI GRATIA REX SCOTORUM.

THIS PLAQUE WAS PLACED HERE TO COMMEMORATE THE SEPULTURE HERE WITHIN THE RUINED BOUNDS OF ST SERF'S PARISH CHURCH, LITTLE KIRKTON, OF THE EMBALMED VISCERAFROM THE BODY OF KING ROBERT THE BRUCE ON OR ABOUT THE THIRD WEEK OF JUNE 1329. THE DYING MONARCH REQUESTED THAT HIS HEART BE TAKEN TO JERUSALEM BY A KNIGHT TEMPLAR IN FULFILMENT OF A SACRED VOW HE HAD MADE EARLIER IN HIS REIGN TO GO ON A CRUSADE TO THE HOLY LAND IN PALESTINE. ON THE SAME DAY AND AT THE HOUR APPOINTED FOR THE ENTOMBMENT OF THE KING IN DUNFERMLINE ABBEY A SIMULTANEOUS SERVICE OF SEPULTURE WAS CONDUCTED WITHIN THE PRECINCTS OF THIS VENERABLE EDIFACE.

Documentation discovered by historian Stuart Smith
was responsible for the plaque being placed at St Serf's in 2001

Tour 1, Glasgow.

Glasgow Cathedral.

The sign of the Spider and internal and external views of Glasgow Cathedral.

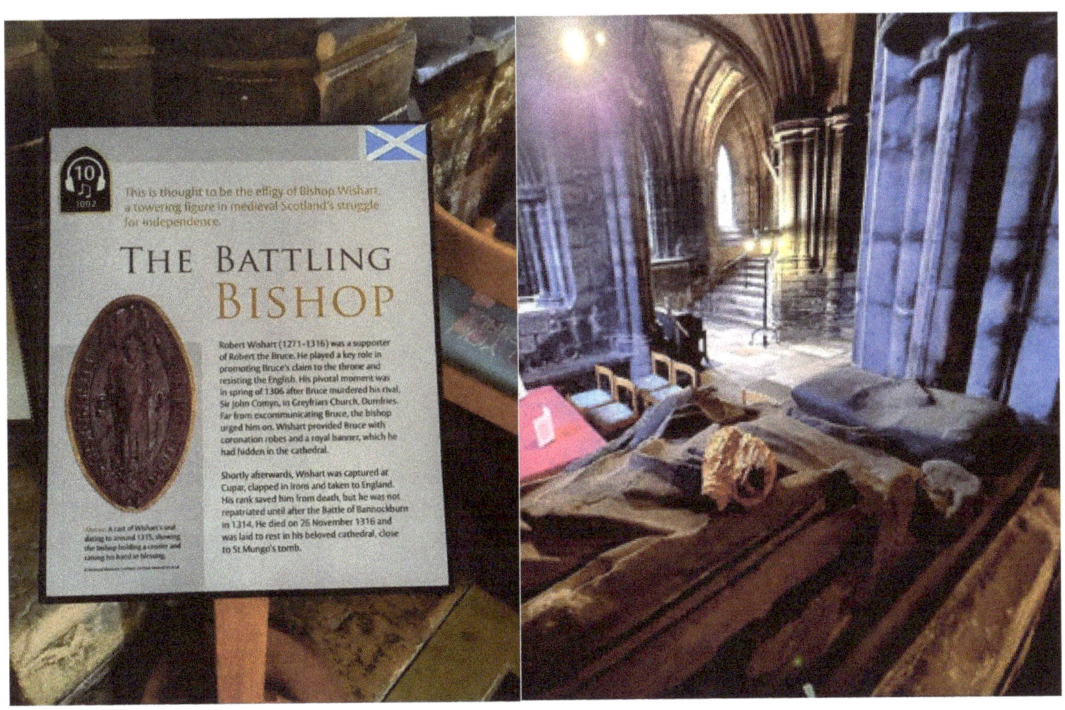

The Bruce Oak Heart on the damaged effigy of Bishop Wishart, supporter of Bruce.

From the Information Board in Glasgow Cathedral:

"This is thought to be the effigy of Bishop Wishart, a towering figure in medieval Scotland's struggle for independence.

THE BATTLING BISHOP

Robert Wishart (1271-1316) was a supporter of Robert the Bruce. He played a key role in promoting Bruce's claim to the throne and resisting the English. His pivotal moment was in spring of 1306 after Bruce murdered his rival, Sir John Comyn, in Greyfriars Church, Dumfries. Far from excommunicating Bruce, the bishop urged him on. Wishart provided Bruce with coronation robes and a royal banner, which he had hidden in the cathedral.

Shortly afterwards, Wishart was captured at Cupar, clapped in irons and taken to England. His rank saved him from death, but he was not repatriated until after the Battle of Bannockbum in 1314. He died on 26 November 1316 and was laid to rest in his beloved cathedral, close to **St Mungo's tomb.** A cast of Wishart's seal dating to around 1315, showing the bishop holding a crozier and raising his hand in blessing. 'Tomb of St Kentigern, (St Mungo).

Top: Effigy of Bishop Wishart viewed from the Nurses Chapel.

Bottom: Patron Saint of Glasgow, St Mungo's Tomb.

Paying respect, monument to William Wallace and the ‘Battle o’ the Bell o’ The Brae’ in the Glasgow Necropolis next to Glasgow Cathedral.

Tour 2, Balloch & Loch Lomond.

St Kessog's RC Church, Balloch, on the southern shore of Loch Lomond.

Local tradition has it that Bruce led his men against the English at Bannockburn, not in the name of St Andrew or St Columba but...*''**in the name of the Blessed Kessog.'***

Bruce Oak Heart, St Kessog's RC Church, Balloch.

The River Leven.

While living in the Vale of Leven, Bruce had his galley rowed up stream on the River Leven to get to his hunting lodge on the western shore of Loch Lomond, at the site of what was the old Youth Hostel - and downstream to **St Serf's Chapel** near the mouth of the river at Dumbarton.

The River Leven from Balloch and the view northwards onto the Lomond Hills, Swans on the riverbank, their symbol was on **Malcolm Earl of Lennox** Heraldry, his castle once stood at the mouth of the river.

Balloch Country Park.

Left: This clearing in woodland near the River Leven is the location of the castle of Bruce's supporter, **Malcolm Earl of Lennox**, only the remains of the defensive ditch, parts of which get flooded, are now visible.

Right: The Bruce Oak Heart held aloft at the ditch by the footbath on the eastern shore of the River Leven, an outflow for Loch Lomond that enters the River Clyde at Dumbarton.

Loch & Ben Lomond.

After the routs of **Methven** and **Dalrigh** the remnants of Bruce's army rowed from the eastern to the western shore of the loch, making their way down southwards they met up with **Malcolm Earl of Lennox** whose castle was situated in the modern day Balloch Country Park.

Looking north to Loch and Ben Lomond from Carman Hill, on the southern flank of the Vale of Leven.

Bruce's Yew: *Stuc an t'lobhairt*, near Firkin Point, Western shore of Loch Lomond.

The tradition that Bruce read to his men on the banks of Loch Lomond originates in 'The Bruce', composed by John Barbour, Archdeacon of Aberdeen, in the 1370s.

Barbour claims that it was the story of Fierabras *('Ferembras' in Barbour's text),* a Muslim lord who converted to Christianity after being defeated in battle by Oliver, one of Charlemagne's Twelve Peers. The relevant passage is found at Bk. 3, ll. 435-66 in the original Scots.

Bruce, with his remaining force of about 200 men after the routs of Methven and Dail-Righ, who had travelled over Loch Lomond in small rowing boats sheltered under an ancient yew tree at Stuc an t'lobhairt, translated as either a Place of Sacrifice or Shelter.

There is an ancient yew tree here at this spot, on a rocky knoll in a private garden. This yew is included in the book Heritage Trees of Scotland (p.192) by Donald Rodger, John Stokes and James Ogilvie (Tree Council 2006).

The entry states how J C Loudon visited in 1837 and recorded a girth of 13 feet (400 cm) at ground level and the height of the yew was 39 feet (12 metres). A 400 cm girth noted almost 200 years ago, would suggest given the habitat conditions of an exposed position and poor nutrient availability, which typically cause slow growth in yew trees, it was probably at the very least 500 years old in Loudon's day. This means it would have been there in Bruce's lifetime.

There is also a depiction of an old postcard from the 1920's which shows the yew to be much reduced in height since Loudon measured it almost a century before. This was the result of drastic pruning undertaken in the interim. It is not much different in appearance 100 years later. The entry goes on to say that in 1998 the girth had increased to 610 cm and "suggests an annual ring width of 2 mm, a reasonable rate of increment for such a slow–growing species in such a harsh environment".

Robert the Bruce is also associated with ancient yews growing on Inchlonaig an isle on Loch Lomond. He harvested yews there to make longbows prior to the battle of Bannockburn in 1314 and planted replacements still to be seen today and are over 700 years old. A sample of these yews had a girth of 517 cm at 100 cm high (SYTHI 2019) showing slow growth rates. This supports Robert the Bruce's yew being contemporary with his lifetime and furthermore it could be over 1,000 years old, as it must have been of some size to shelter so many men over 700 years ago.

This ancient yew tree, a true and hardy survivor, may well be a shadow of its former self. However this doughty yew has evidence to support the real possibility that it could indeed have served Robert the Bruce and his men on their campaign to regain the freedom of the nation. Although the link with Robert the Bruce has to remain a matter of belief rather than provable historical fact, nevertheless, if ever a tree deserved the status of being an Ancient Monument then surely this yew tree does.

Left: **The Bruce Yew** at 'Stuc an t'lobhairt' near **Firkin Point**, Loch Lomondside

Right: View looking down onto the southern islands of Loch Lomond from **Ben Dhubh.**

Local tradition has Bruce using one of these islands, **Inchlonaig** to plant **Yew Trees** for his archers. Inchlonaig is the northernmost of the large islands on Loch Lomond and lies west of the village of **Luss.**

It has an ancient connection with people as traces of human habitation date back to 5000 BC. Inchlonaig is said to mean ***'isle of the yew trees'*** in almost all sources.

Prior to the battle of Bannockburn Bruce harvested yews from various locations to provide longbows for his forces including **Ardchattan Priory** in the highlands as well as Inchlonaig.

Although not used to the same extent found in English armies, archers were significant in Scottish military tactics at the time and played a decisive part in the battle – as did the yew trees which provided the longbows.

Some accounts state that Bruce planted yews on Inchlonaig some years before Bannockburn and it was these yews which were harvested, however a yew a decade or so old could not yield any wood suitable for a military quality longbow.

So it would appear that old and probably ancient yews were harvested and then replaced.]

Bruce Oak Arrowhead Medallion.

St Kessog's Church, Luss, Loch Lomondside.

St Kessog's Church, note Viking 'hogback' grave marker bottom right of picture.

Effigy of St Kessog with Bruce Oak Heart.

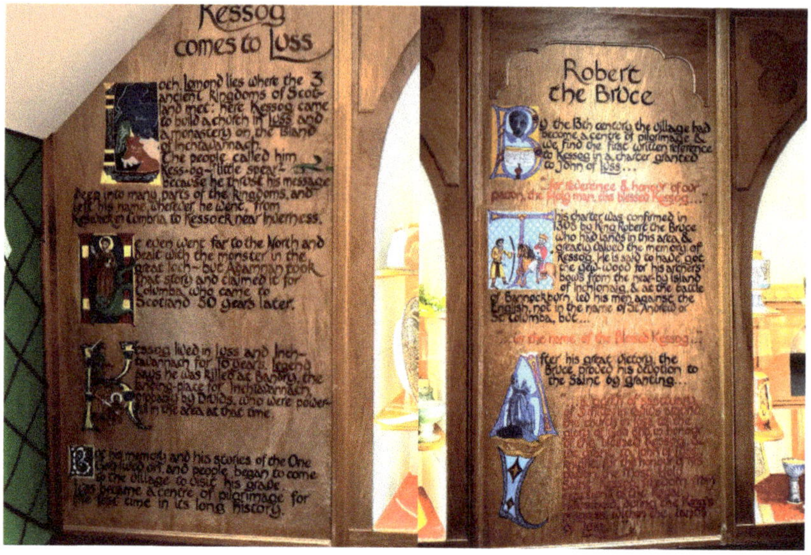

Information Panels in Luss Heritage Centre containing the following information:

Panel 1. Kessog comes to Luss.

Loch Lomond lies where the 3 ancient Kingdoms of Scotland met: here Kessog came to build a church in Luss and a monastery on the island of Inchtavannach
The people called him Kess-og – 'little spear' because he thrust his message across into many parts of the kingdoms, and left his name wherever he went, from Keswick in Combria to Kessock near Inverness.
He even went for to the North and dealt with the monster in the great loch - but Adamnan took that story and claimed it for Columba who came to Scotland 50 years later.
Kessog lived in Luss and Inchtavannach (island on Loch Lomond) for 10 years Legend says he was killed at Bandry, the landing-place for Inchavannach, probably by Druids, who were powerful in the area at that time.
But his memory and his stories of the One God lived on, and people began to come to the village to visit his grave. Luss became & centre of pilgrimage for first time in its long history.

Panel 2. Robert the Bruce.

By the 13th century the village had become a centre of pilgrimage and we find the first written reference to Kessog in a charter granted to John of Luss.

"...for reverence & honour of our patron, the Holy man, the blessed Kessog..."

This charter was confirmed in 1308 by Robert the Bruce who had lands in this area & greatly valued the memory of Kessog.

He is said to have got the yew wood for his archers' bows from the nearby island of Inchlonaig & at the battle Bannockburn led his men against the English, not in the name of St Andrew or St Columba but....

"in the name of the Blessed Kessog..."

After his great victory the Bruce proved his devotion to the Saint by granting...

"A garth of sanctuary of 3 miles radius around the church in Luss to the glory of God and in honour of the blessed Kessog, and we grant to John of Luss, knight for the honour of his patron, the Most Holy St Kessog freedom from exactions of the royal household, during the Kings progress within the lands of Luss."

Tour 3, Up to Inverness, and beyond to Tain.

Methven, 19th June 1306, Rout of Bruce's Force.

Bruce was crowned King of Scots by **Bishop William de Lamberton** at Scone, near Perth, on **Palm Sunday 25 March 1306.** Enraged by the killing of **John the Red Comyn, Lord of Badenoch** by Bruce and his followers at Dumfries and Bruce's coronation, Edward I of England named Aymer de Valence, Earl of Pembroke, and special lieutenant for Scotland.

Pembroke moved quickly, and by the middle of summer he had made his base at Perth, along with **Henry Percy** and **Robert Clifford** with an army of about 3000 men drawn from the northern counties. Edward I gave orders that **no mercy was to be granted** and all taken in arms were to be **executed without trial**.

It is possible that the order of "no mercy" had not reached King Robert because he resorted to chivalric tradition and called on de Valence to come out from the walls of Perth and do battle.

De Valence, who had the reputation of an honourable man, made the excuse that it was too late in the day to do battle and said he would accept the challenge on the following day. The king bivouacked his army some six miles away in some woods that were on high ground near the River Almond. At about dusk as the Bruce's army made camp and many disarmed, the army of de Valence fell upon them in a surprise attack.

The king unhorsed the Earl of Pembroke in the first onslaught but was unhorsed himself and nearly captured by **Sir Philip Mowbray** only to be saved by **Sir Christopher Seton**. Outnumbered and taken by surprise, the king's force had no chance. Bruce was **twice more unhorsed and twice more rescued**. At the last, a small force of Scottish knights including **James Douglas, Neil Campbell, Edward Bruce, John de Strathbogie, Earl of Atholl, Gilbert de Haye** and the king formed a phalanx to break free and were forced to flee in a shattering defeat, leaving many of the king's most loyal followers dead or soon to be executed.

Those captured during the battle included **Alexander Fraser, David de Inchmartin, Hugh de Haye, John Somerville, Alexander Scrymgeour, the royal standard bearer, Thomas de Randolph, Bruce's nephew and Hugh, Bruce's chaplain.**

Setting up the hill from the Methven Den Car Park.

Left: Path up to the Battle Stone. Right: Stone marker for the path through the Den of Methven.

Bruce Oak Heart with Stone from Teba,
where Sir James Douglas fell in battle carrying the King's Heart.

Left: This burn in the Den of Methven may well have been the water supply for Bruce's troops.

Right: The grassy slope is on the eastern side of the Burn. Again, this may well have been wooded at the time of the battle. Aymer de Valence would likely have attacked from above, pressing down onto Bruce's camp from the north.

The Information Board reads:

The Battle of Methven took place at Methven in 1306 during the Wars of Scottish Independence.
Robert the Bruce, The King, arrived at Perth on Sunday but the English refused to fight on the Sabbath.
The Scots retired only a few miles to nearby Methven, where Bruce made camp for the night.
Before dawn on the 19th of June, his army was surprised by the English, led by the Earl of Pembroke, whom Bruce trusted as a fellow knight and would have given his word to make battle the following day.
Bruce failed to take the precaution of placing pickets around the camp. His entire army was routed.
After this experience, he borrowed a page from the book of William Wallace and switched to guerrilla warfare which the latter had usually preferred.

Cholliebhrochain, Blair Atholl, Perth & Kinross.

We are in the realm of legend here, the name *Coillebhrochain* translates from Gaelic as ***'Wood of the Porridge or Brose'*** indicative of local folklore that Bruce was given refuge here in 1306 after his defeat at the battle of Methven. Here he is said to have been given a form of Atholl Brose, (traditionally mixing oatmeal, water or milk, honey, whisky - and sometimes cream).

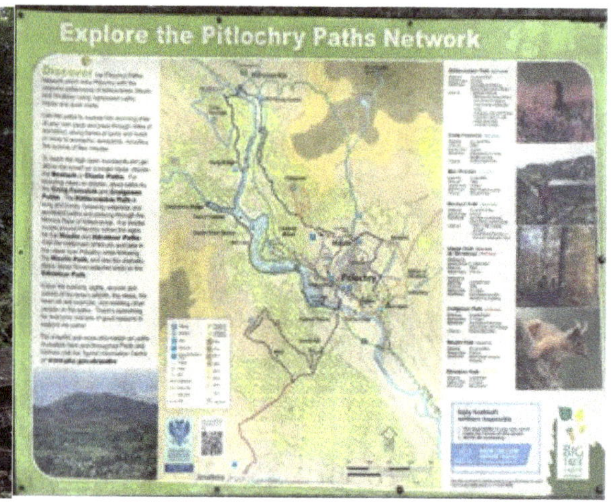

Left: Garry Bridge Car Park, (south of Killiekrankie on the B8019), start of the Linn of Tummel Walk to Cholliebhrochain.

Turning southwards under the Garry Bridge towards Cholliebhrochain.

Left: Bungee Jumping Platform cage under the Garry Bridge. Right: Path leading up to Cholliebhrochain.

Mist covered Perthshire Hills and the approach to the memorial.

The Bruce Oak Heart at the memorial to Bruce taking shelter at this spot after Methven.

Left: 'That which does not kill us makes us stronger', the Lion Rampant flies again after Methven.

Right: Path heading back to Garry Bridge car park, *Caution Wet Planks!*

Clan Donnachaidh Centre, Bruar, Perthshire.

Clan Donnachaidh Centre and miniature sculpture of the Bannockburn Monument to Bruce.

Clan Robertson is correctly known as ***Clan Donnachaidh*** – the only Scottish clan that still uses its Gaelic name as standard.

Its principal surnames are **Robertson, Duncan** and **Reid**, found in large numbers in the clan heartland in Perthshire and the neighbouring counties - but there are also many other septs.

The clan's first recognised chief, **Donnchaidh Reamhar**, *(Stout Duncan – stout in battle rather than belly)*, son of **Andrew de Atholia**, *(Andrew of Atholl)*, was a minor land-owner and leader of a kin-group around Dunkeld in Highland Perthshire and, as legend has it, he was an enthusiastic and faithful supporter of Bruce and is believed to have looked after Bruce after the **Battle of Methven** in 1306.

He called his son and heir **Robert** very possibly after the King. Clan Donnachaidh is traditionally listed among the clans present at the Battle of Bannockburn in 1314.

His descendants became known as the **Duncansons,** (Clann Dhònnchaidh, "Children of Duncan"). Duncan is believed to have been killed at the Battle of Neville's Cross 17 October 1346 and was succeeded by Robert, from whom the **Clan Robertson** takes its name.

Below extract from www.clandonnachaidhpnw.com:

In 1306 Bruce was crowned at Scone and soon after was routed at the battle of Methven.
*He, his queen, and a few followers escaped into Atholl and, again according to legend, were received by Duncan. Duncan was thought to have had his stronghold in a castle on the island in **Loch Tummel,** which was submerged in 1950 when the loch was raised by five metres by a hydro-electric dam, and Bruce took refuge in the the **Wood of Kynachan** just a couple of miles to the west.*

*A ford on the Tummel, now beneath **Dunalastair Water**, was the **King's ford.** The **King's Hall** was in the woods to the south and the **Queen's Pool** was a little further downstream. Strong tradition tells of an unrecorded battle between Lochs Tummel and Rannoch at this time. **Innerhadden** was where the battle started, **Dalchosnie** next door means field of fighting; **Glen Sassunn** is the **Glen of the southerners,** the route taken by the enemy troops.*

The result was a victory thanks to the women of the Clan who supported their menfolk by filling stockings with stones and using them as clubs to devastating effect.

With Clan Donnachaidh by his side, the king ventured west and was defeated at ***Dalrigh*** *(the field of the king) near Tyndrum by the Macdougalls of Lorne and retired back to* ***Strathtummel.***

In this battle the king lost the brooch with which he pinned his cloak and this is still in the possession of the victor's descendants. Eight years later the Clan went down to Bannockburn to fight alongside Bruce to defeat the English and make him undisputed king of Scots.

Bannockburn, of course, is the seminal battle in the fight for Scots independence from England. As a result every clan wishes to claim that it was part of Bruce's army.

The earliest written reference to the participation of the clans seems not come until 1822, when the historian ***David Stewart of Garth*** *listed twenty one Highland chiefs that were there, but he gives no source for the information.*

There is strong logic that Clan Donnachaidh would have been at Bannockburn. Clan Donnachaidh is said to have been a little late for the conflict, and were part of the contingent that came down from Gillies Hill at the decisive moment of the battle and these reinforcements tipped the balance in Bruce's favour.

On the bare framework of this tradition an elaborate account of the Clan's involvement in the battle has been constructed which ends with the victorious king declaring

'Hitherto ye have been called the sons of Duncan,
but henceforth ye shall be called my children.'

This explanation of the origin of ***Robert-son*** *as the Clan's primary surname actually predates its first use by well over a century. The Clan had several more encounters with the Macdougalls. The only record of one was written down by Ewen Macdougall, Clerk to the Earl of Breadalbane at Taymouth, in the 1820s and describes the aftermath of a cattle raid or creach against Clan Donnachaidh.*

The Macdougalls were tracked west and the two forces met in Glen Orchy 'where they fought bitterly, the Rannoch men were slain and their Chief fled with difficulty. The slain were buried and the cairns are still called ***Cairn nan Rannoch****, or Rannoch Men's Cairns, and their arms cast into a small Loch near the Cairns called* ***Lochan nan Arn****.'*

It seems likely that this is a traditional local interpretation of Bruce's defeat at Tyndrum after which the losers' weapons were also said to have been thrown into the loch. If so, it would indicate that the bulk of Bruce's army were Clan Donnachaidh men, and that the ordinary Macdougall warriors were more pleased to have defeated them than the king.

The monarch must have been a remote figure to most people, intent on consolidating his national position. Duncan's followers were local rivals against whom clashes must have been frequent. However with Duncan at its head the Clan was usually on the winning side. It is possible that his most famous meeting with the Macdougalls is an amalgam of several skirmishes, particularly since the date given by one source of 1338 would make him past his prime for legendary feats of agility.

They sent an army into Atholl and Duncan, disguised as a beggar, entered the enemy camp to scout it out. His cover was penetrated and he had to flee for his life. He chopped down one of his pursuers and then jumped across the chasm of the ***River Errochty*** *to escape. The spot is now beneath the dammed Loch Errochty so the distance, variously reported between 11 and 16 feet, cannot be confirmed.*

His Gaelic name Donnachd Reamhar (pronounced 'rav-ar') means literally Fat Duncan, but a gravitationally-challenged warrior in his mid-fifties is unlikely to have managed such a leap. ***'Robust'*** *or* ***'stout'*** *would surely be a more accurate translation. Another of his sobriquets was* ***Gaisgeach Mor Fea-Chorie*** *- the great hero of Fea Corrie. The corrie, a remote cleft in the hills west of* ***Trinafour****, was the muster point for Duncan's warriors before any campaign. It, too, is submerged beneath Loch Errochty.*

The Bruce Oak Heart atop the display cabinet containing the Clach na Brataich.

The **Clach na Brataich** – the Stone of the Standard – the charm stone of the Clan Donnachaidh, one version of the stone's story is that it was unearthed ahead of the battle of Bannockburn. At first light, the chief's standard was pulled from the ground and with it the stone appeared.

Inverness.

Bridge over the River Ness, coloured lights reflecting the fight for freedom that continues in modern times.

Left: The modern day Inverness Castle.
Right: The Bruce, (Oak Heart), once again assails its slopes.

A succession of castles have stood on this site since 1057. The castle is said to have been built by Malcolm III of Scotland. The first Inverness Castle was partially destroyed by Bruce.

The Treaty of Inverness:

Extract from the ***Battle of Bannockburn Experience*** *Facebook page:*

In 29th October 1312, King Robert I of Scotland was in Inverness.
Here, he ratified a treaty with two representatives of King Håkon V of Norway – Berner de Berkerey and Ivar son of Olaf, canon of Bergen and Orkney – formally renewing and normalising relations between Scotland and Norway.

Though the terms of the treaty were straightforward and uncontroversial, the document is nonetheless significant in that it was the ***first major diplomatic success of King Robert's reign.***

One of the main themes of Scottish history during the thirteenth-century had been the expansion of royal power westwards into the Hebrides, which had been part of the Kingdom of Norway since about the ninth-century.

In 1266, as part of the ***Treaty of Perth****, King Magnús IV of Norway had formally ceded the Western Isles and the Isle of Man to King Alexander III of Scotland.*

In return, the Scots agreed to pay 100 marks annually, to be delivered at St Magnus Cathedral on Orkney. However, the succession crisis that followed King Alexander's death in 1286 and war with England since 1296 had disrupted these payments, or at the very least given the Scots a convenient excuse to stop making them.

Scoto-Norwegian relations had also been undermined by reported raids on Shetland by Scottish pirates, some of whom had even captured the Norwegian seneschal (i.e., steward) of Orkney and extorted an enormous ransom for his release. On another occasion, a Scottish squire named Patrick Mowat had been imprisoned, beaten, and robbed by the Norwegian royal bailiff on Orkney. On another, some merchants from St Andrews were imprisoned on arrival in Norway and had £600 of their goods confiscated.

Most Scottish governments had been too distracted by the on-going conflict with England to pay much attention to relations with Norway. Bruce on the other hand was unusually well-equipped to make some headway in the arena of Scoto-Norwegian diplomacy.

By 1312, he had achieved sufficient control over the northern parts of his kingdom to guarantee that the local lords would enforce whatever settlement the king reached with his Norwegian counterpart.

Moreover, his (probably elder) sister Isabella had married King Eirik II of Norway in 1293. After her husband's death in 1299, Isabella had remained in Norway and enjoyed good relations with her brother-in-law Håkon V.

There is also some evidence of her corresponding with her family in Scotland, and although none of this directly relates to events in 1312, historian Randi Wærdahl has convincingly argued that Isabella may have used her influence at Håkon's court to assist her brother's negotiations over the Treaty of Inverness.

Bruce is unlikely to have visited Norway in person, and so any discussions that took place in Norway were probably undertaken by Bruce's chancellor Bernard, Abbot of Arbroath.

The terms of the final treaty were, in and of themselves, largely unremarkable and in effect amounted to little more than a restatement of the terms originally agreed in 1266.

The Scots once again committed themselves to paying the 100-mark annual rent for the Hebrides, and the payments did indeed resume (only to be halted again shortly after King Robert's death).

No mention was made of the arrears the Scots technically owed for the years they had missed, but the Scottish crown agreed to fork out a further 600 marks in compensation for the mistreatment of the Norwegian seneschal.

In return, the Norwegian crown promised to reimburse the St Andrews merchants for their impounded goods, and both sides exchanged rather more vague promises to investigate the raiding of Shetland and the imprisonment of the hapless Mowat. Bruce had brought with him to Inverness a significant following of local potentates.

Their job on the day was to witness the agreement the king was making and reassure King Håkon's representatives that the terms would be respected. Going forward, their role would be to ensure that the terms were adhered to day-to-day.

They included ***William, earl of Ross, Thomas Randolph, earl of Moray****,* ***David Strathbogie, earl of Atholl****, the leading secular figures in the northern, central, and southern Highlands respectively. Randolph and Strathbogie were also Bruce's nephews (Strathbogie by marriage).*

The king was also accompanied by ***Henry Cheyne, bishop of Aberdeen****,* ***David de Moravia, bishop of Moray****,* ***Thomas of Dundee, bishop of Ross****, and* ***Farquhar Bellejambe, bishop of Caithness,*** *adding the moral force of northern Scotland's spiritual leaders to the commitments Bruce was making.*

The Treaty of Inverness as it has become known serves as a powerful demonstration of Robert Bruce's talents as a statesman. In material terms, the treaty clearly favoured the Norwegians.

Yet the financial burden of the 'annual' was minor compared to the symbolic significance of the agreement.

In reaching this accommodation with Bruce, as opposed to say King Edward II of England, King Håkon was formally recognising Robert as King of Scots.

For Håkon, this was perhaps little more than a pragmatic acknowledgement of the fact that if he wanted peaceful relations with the northern parts of Scotland, Bruce was the only figure with the temporal power to guarantee this in practice.

For Robert, it was a potent vindication of his success in bringing a substantial portion of the realm under his control, and it could furthermore be used to apply diplomatic pressure to other European rulers to recognise his rights as well.

After all, if King Håkon was willing to publicly acknowledge Bruce, why shouldn't the King of France? (Philippe IV had indeed been styling Robert as King of Scots in private since at least 1309) Why not the pope? Why not the King of England for that matter?

With the Treaty of Inverness, we thus see King Robert making minor material concessions in order to achieve his wider diplomatic goals.

St Andrews Cathedral, Inverness.

Inverness Episcopal Cathedral is the Mother Church of the Diocese of Moray, Ross and Caithness.

Kessock Bridge, connecting Inverness with the Black Isle & the far north.

The bridge is named after ***St Kessog*** who Bruce was said to have prayed to after the rout of Dalrigh and before the Battle of Bannockburn.

The Kessock Bridge is a cable-stayed bridge across the Beauly Firth, an inlet of the

Moray Firth, between the village of North Kessock and the City of Inverness

Tain, St Duthac's Chapel.

Left: Looking northwards onto Cromarty Bridge from the Black Isle.
Right: Directions to St Duthus, (Duthuc's), Chapel.

Left: Lion Emblem above entrance to Tain Sherriff Court.
Right: Clan Ross Visitor Centre, William II Earl of Ross handed the Bruce Womenfolk over to Edward I after they sought sanctuary in St Duthac's, possibly while heading further north to the Orkneys – and perhaps even onto Norway.

Locally, St Duthac's is known as *'St Duthus'.*

The Bruce Oak Heart, having travelled from the Vale of Leven to Jerusalem now reaches Tain.

Capture of the Bruce Women and execution of their Escort.

In **August 1306** King Robert split his party after the defeat at Methven on the 19th June; while he headed west he sent **his daughter Marjorie and wife Elizabeth** to the north-east, possibly hoping they could escape to Orkney and onto Norway, where his sister, Isabel, was Queen.

Accompanying Elizabeth and Marjorie were King Robert's other 2 sisters, **Christian and Mary**, and also **Isabella MacDuff, Countess of Buchan**, who had crowned Robert at Scone.
They were escorted by **John of Strathbogie, Earl of Atholl**, and Robert's younger brother, **Sir Nigel / Niall Bruce.** By **September 1306**, the women and their escort had reached **Kildrummy Castle** in Aberdeenshire; where Edward's forces caught up with them. While **Sir Nigel / Niall Bruce** and the garrison stoically attempted to hold off the English, **John of Strathbogie, Earl of Atholl** escaped with the women of the court.
Having made it to the far north of Scotland, they were apprehended at **St Duthac's Chapel, Tain**, north of Inverness, by **William II, Earl of Ross**, a supporter of the Comyns. Kildrummy had fallen in the meantime after the castle was set alight by a traitor who was bribed with as much gold as he could carry.

The traitor was said to have been rewarded with molten gold poured down his throat, whether true or not it may well have been used as propaganda against any Scot siding with the English. Sir Nigel / Niall Bruce and the Kildrummy garrison were handed over to the English and executed; Sir Nigel / Niall suffered hanging, drawing and quartering at **Berwick.**

The **Earl of Atholl and the Bruce women, along with the Countess of Buchan**, who had been captured in Tain, were sent south to **King Edward I.** When they reached London, the **Earl of Atholl** suffered the same fate as Sir Nigel / Niall, the first Earl to ever suffer a traitor's execution.

Although Edward did not order the executions of the womenfolk, it cannot be said he treated them kindly. They were used to set an example; a demonstration of the price of rebellion against him.

For **Mary Bruce and Isabella MacDuff, Countess of Buchan**, he ordered the construction of **iron cages**.

Isabella, who had set the crown of Scotland on Robert the Bruce's head, was imprisoned in one such cage suspended high from the walls of **Berwick castle**; open the elements and the mockery of the people of Berwick.

"Let her be closely confined in an abode of stone and iron made in the shape of a cross, and let her be hung up out of doors in the open air at Berwick, that both in life and after her death, she may be a spectacle and eternal reproach to travellers."

She was imprisoned in this cage for four years. The other Bruce women captured with her suffered similar fates at various locations throughout England. Later, when Bruce was gaining support, **Isabella was moved to the Carmelite friary at Berwick**. Bruce's female relatives were potentially valuable hostages, and the English did not want them to die of ill-treatment.

The last clear mention of her is being transferred again in 1313 but her eventual fate is uncertain. The same form of imprisonment was ordered for **Mary Bruce at Roxburgh Castle.** Mary was eventually released in 1314. She married twice and had a single son, **John Campbell, Earl of Atholl**. She died around 1323.

Christian Bruce, (whose husband Sir Christopher Seton, had been hanged, drawn and beheaded at Dumfries as a traitor), was ordered to be confined at a **Convent at Sixhills in Lincolnshire**; while **Elizabeth de Burgh** was confined to various manors and treated less harshly due to her father being the **Earl of Ulster** and his friendship with Edward I.

For **Marjorie Bruce**, these events must have been terrifying. Edward ordered her confined in an iron cage in the Tower of London, which happened to have a zoo of exotic animals, where no one was to speak to her.
Whether Edward relented of his own free will, or was advised against such treatment of a child the order was rescinded and she was confined to a **Convent at Watton in Yorkshire.**

There, the young Marjory lived, virtually alone, for 8 years. She was released after Bannockburn in 1314, when she was 17, in exchange for English prisoners held by the Scots.
Robert the Bruce's resounding victory over Edward I's son and successor, Edward II, in the 1314 battle meant Bruce was finally in a position to insist on the return of his queen, daughter, sisters and the Countess of Buchan.

With so many English nobles taken prisoner, the women were the price demanded in the exchange of hostages. On Marjorie's return to Scotland, King Robert almost immediately set about arranging her marriage. With the queen not yet having produced a child, the now-17-year-old Marjorie was needed to produce an heir for the Bruce dynasty.

Just 5 years older the Marjorie, **Walter Stewart,** the wealthy and powerful **6th High Steward of Scotland** was the ideal candidate as a husband. Walter had distinguished himself as a commander at the Battle of Bannockburn, and was the man entrusted by Bruce to bring his family home for their English captivity.
Walter and Marjorie were married shortly after, with Marjorie's dowry including the Barony of Bathgate in West Lothian. Whatever happiness, if any, Marjorie derived from the marriage, however, was short-lived.

In 1316, whilst heavily pregnant, she fell from her horse when out riding near Paisley Abbey. Going into premature labour, Marjorie was taken to the Abbey, where she was delivered of a son, Robert, on 2nd March 1316. It is possible that Robert was delivered by caesarean section as his mother was close to death. Marjorie survived the birth by just a few hours and died the same day. She died at the age of barely 19, having spent close to half her life in near-solitary confinement.

Fortrose Cathedral.

In recognition of the efforts of other Scots Patriots, the Bruce Oak Heart was taken to Fortrose Cathedral, the burial site of **Sir Andrew Moray**, Wallace's Co-Commander at the Battle of Stirling Bridge, 11th Sept 1297.

The Bruce Oak Heart rests awhile at Fortrose Cathedral.

Although William Wallace is remembered as Scotland's national hero, it was Moray who raised the standard to mark the start of the War for Independence in 1297.

Moray was responsible for leading the Northern Rising against the rule of Edward I

He raised the standard at Ormond Castle, Avoch, overlooking the Moray Firth, and led an army to successfully regain control of the north.

Urquhart Castle.

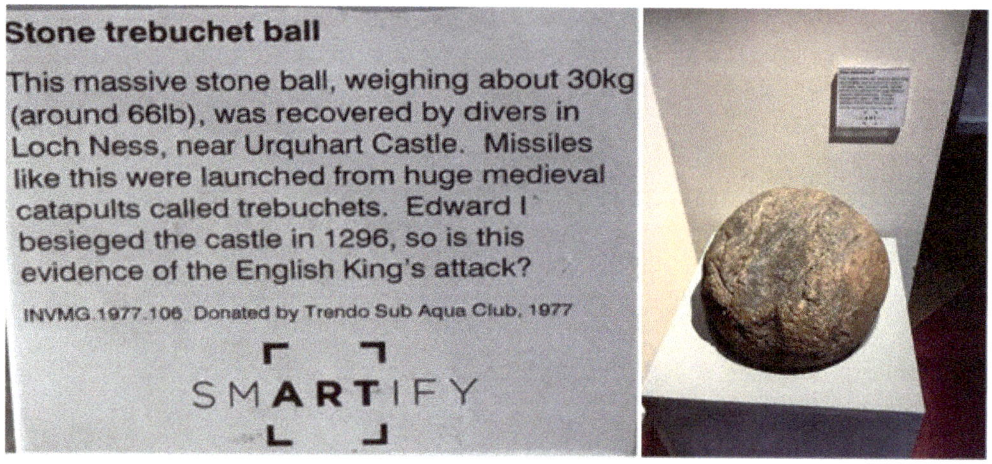

Inverness Museum, Stone Trebuchet Ball found at Urquhart Castle, Loch Ness.

Urquhart Castle, near Drumnadrochit.

Note the arm of a replica trebuchet sticking out from the trees on the right.

The first documented record of Urquhart Castle was in 1296 when it was captured by Edward I who appointed Sir William Fitz Warin as constable to hold the castle for the English.
In 1297 he was ambushed by **Sir Andrew Moray** while returning from Inverness, and Moray subsequently laid siege to the castle, launching an unsuccessful night attack.
The English were ousted soon after; in 1298 Urquhart was again controlled by the Scots.
In 1303 Sir Alexander de Forbes failed to hold off another English assault. This time Edward installed Alexander Comyn, (brother of John The Red Comyn), as governor, as the family had sided with the English against Bruce. Following the killing of the John The Red Comyn in 1306, Bruce completed his defeat of the Comyns when he marched through the Great Glen in 1307, taking the castles of Inverlochy, Urquhart and Inverness. After this time Urquhart became a royal castle, held for the crown by a series of constables.

Commando Memorial, Spean Bridge.

In recognition of the 'Commando like' tactics adopted by Bruce and his Commanders James Douglas and Thomas Randolph, the Bruce Oak Heart was taken to the memorial at Spean Bridge.

Ben Nevis, under cloud.

Scotland's highest point from Neptune's Staircase, Caledonian Canal.

Inverlochy Castle, Fort William.

Castle of the Comyns.

Inverlochy Castle was built in about 1280 by the 'Red' Comyns, lords of Badenoch and Lochaber, to command the southern end of the Great Glen. The Comyns were one of the most powerful families in Scotland in the 1200s, with estates ranging across the country.

The Comyns remained loyal to King John Balliol even after his overthrow by Edward I of England in 1296. **Sir John Comyn of Badenoch and Lochaber** died peacefully at Inverlochy in 1300. Six years later, his son, also named John, was killed in Dumfries by Bruce.

When Bruce seized the throne in 1306, he sparked a civil war and had to make the overthrow of the Comyns a priority. In 1308 he defeated them at Inverurie, Aberdeenshire. Thereafter Inverlochy, along with other Comyn castles, fell into Bruce's hands.

WELCOME TO
INVERLOCHY

The Lion Rampant, emblem of Scots Monarchs, at Inverlochy.

Heading south from Inverlochy Castle through Glencoe.

Battle of Dalrigh, near Tyndrum.

Dalrigh: 'Field of The King'. A rout for Bruce's army, the 2nd in a row, this time by the Pro-Comyn faction of Clan MacDougall, Bruce's army already shattered after Methven. Bruce would survive this battle and escape with his life. Just 2 years after the battle of Dalrigh, he would have his revenge on the McDougall's when his army met the McDougall's again at the Battle of the Pass of Brander.

Bruce would go on to divide up the McDougall's lands and share them between those who had remained loyal to him.

Left: Looking south towards the Crianlarich Hills.

Right: The track towards the **'Lochan of the Lost Sword'** Stone Marker.

River Fillan, on the West Highland Way.

The Sword Marker Stone and Bench are conveniently set either side of the track on the West Highland Way – however the Lochan itself is further away and they appear to have been placed here for the benefit of those who walk on the way.

River Fillan – its banks were the scene of hard fighting and the loss of Bruce's Cloak and Brooch at the hands of the MacDougalls.

After Dalrigh, Bruce and his men 'took to the heather'
- southwards via Loch Lomond and into the lands of Malcolm Earl of Lennox.

St Fillans Chapel, near to Dalrigh.

River Fillan, Strathfillan & the Crianlarich Hills.

Fillan of Munster lived from about **695 to about 770,** he was an Irish missionary who is venerated in several different parts of Scotland. Fillan was the son of **Feriach (Feriacus regulus of Monchestre, who possibly is the same person as Feradach, grandson of Artúr of Dál Riata)** and **Princess Caintigern (Kentigerna)**, daughter of **Cellach Cualann**, King of Leinster.

He received the monastic habit at the Abbey of Fintán of Taghmon in Wexford and came to Scotland from Ireland in 717 as a hermit along with his Irish princess-mother who came to be known as **St. Kentigerna,** and her brother, Fillan's Irish prince-uncle who was later to become **St. Comgán** .

They settled at Loch Duich on Scotland's north west coast. A degree of uncertainty surrounds the life of Fillan and after spending some time with his uncle Saint Comgan at Lochalsh, where **Killilan** *(Kilfillan),* a few miles north east of Dornie bears his name, the saint devoted himself to the evangelization of the district of Perthshire, around Strath Fillan, which is called after him, and where he was greatly venerated.

The widowed St. Kentigerna is said to have ended up living as a hermit, first in Strath Fillan, then in the Lennox, on the island of **Inchcailloch** on Loch Lomond. The name Fillan probably means ***"little wolf*'** in Irish / Gaeilge, being formed on a diminutive of faol, an old word for the animal. In Irish/Gaeilge the name Faolán is pronounced 'Fway-lawn'.

Legend has it that, while St. Fillan was either ploughing fields, or his ox was pulling materials near Killin, a wolf took the life of the ox and thus Fillan could not continue. A '***geis'*** was put on the ox, which meant the wolf had to take the place of the ox and do its work. The story may be considered more of a parable than historical truth, but the connection with the origins of Fillan's name remains obvious.

St Fillan is also closely associated with the village of **Killin**, where he is believed to have established a mill and he was remembered in an exhibition in the **Breadalbane Folklore Centre** until it closed. At the centre are a set of river stones which were believed to have been given healing powers by St. Fillan.

A particular sequence of movements of an appropriate stone around the afflicted area was believed to result in a cure as each stone cured a specific part of the body. He is also associated with the village of **St Fillans**, at the west end of **Loch Earn**. Until 1817 it was called **Port of Lochearn or Meikleport**, but renamed by the landowner because of his belief that St Fillan had converted the local Picts to Christianity.

Later in life St Fillan is said to have lived as a hermit in a cave at **Pittenweem**, which today has a shrine to him. He also established churches (or had early churches established by others dedicated to him) in **Galloway** and on **Islay.** St. Fillan was the abbot of a monastery in Fife before retiring to Glen Dochart and Strathfillan near Tyndrum in Perthshire.

St. Fillan was credited with powers such as the healing of the sick and also possessed a luminous glow from his left arm which he used to study and copy Sacred Scripture in the dark. At an Augustinian priory near the modern day **Kirkton Farm** along to the West Highland Way, the priory's lay abbot, who was its superior in the reign of **William the Lion**, held high rank in the Scottish kingdom.

This monastery was restored by **Robert the Bruce**, and became a cell of the abbey of canons regular at **Inchaffray Abbey**. The new foundation received a grant from King Robert, in gratitude for the aid which he was supposed to have obtained from a relic of the saint on the eve of the great victory over King Edward II's army at the Battle of Bannockburn. **The** 'Mayne' was an arm bone, now lost, enclosed in a silver reliquary or casket. The success of the Scots at Bannockburn was attributed to the presence of the arm of Saint Fillan, which was borne by its custodian, the **Abbot of Inchaffray**, on the field of battle.

Legend has it that **King Robert I** requested the bone be brought to the Bannockburn battle site. The **Deoir,** *(gaelic for Dewar),* hereditary keeper of the relic, and the **Abbot of Inchaffray Abbey l**eft the bone behind and brought only the reliquary because they didn't want the relic to fall into English possession.

On the eve of the Bannockburn battle, as the *Deoir,* the abbot and King Robert knelt in prayer, a noise came from the reliquary. As they looked at the reliquary as the door opened and the bone fell to the floor.

The Bruce won the battle the next day and he established a monastery to thank St. Fillan for the victory.

The saint's original chapel was up river, slightly northwest of the abbey and adjacent to a deep body of water which became known as St. Fillan's 'Holy Pool', believed to have been blessed by St Fillan and effective in curing the mentally ill as a result.

As a result of this traditionally held view he became the patron saint of the mentally ill. In Strathfillan are the ruins of Saint Fillan's chapel, and nearby is the **Holy Pool**, in which people with mental health issues were bathed in order to obtain a cure by the saint's intercession. *Sir Walter Scott* refers to it in his novel ***'Marmion'.*** Other relics include:

- **The Quigrich**, or saint's staff, crosier, also known as the *Coygerach,* is also one of the sacred battle-ensigns of Scotland and said to have been present at Bannockburn. It was long in the possession of a family of the name of **Jore or Dewar**, who were its hereditary guardians in the Middle Ages. The Dewars, (Deoiradh), certainly had it in their custody during 1428, and their right was formally recognized by **King James III** in 1487.
  The head of the crosier, which is of silver-gilt with a smaller one of bronze enclosed within it, is in the National Museum of Scotland.

- **The Bernane**, St. Fillan's bronze bell. A cast bronze bell is also preserved in the National Museum of Scotland and was placed over a sufferer's head during healing rituals in order to heal such afflictions as migraine headaches and more. During the Middle Ages the bell was kept in the care of **Deoiradh** at several Glen Dochart farms.

Legend has it that the bell would come to St. Fillan when called. One day a visitor who was unused to seeing bells flying through the air was startled and shot it with an arrow, causing a crack. The Bernane was used in the **coronation of King James IV at Scone on 24 June 1488.**

Another story came about only in the early 19th century, concerning an English tourist who stole the bell. The bell was recovered by **Bishop Forbes** of the Episcopalian Diocese of Brechin 70 years later, in 1869, who had it placed in the Scottish National Museum in Edinburgh for safe keeping.

St. Fillan of Munster is commemorated on 3 February, and was specially venerated at Cluain Mavscua, County Westmeath, Ireland, and at the villages of Houston and Kilellan, Renfrewshire, Scotland and so early as the 8th or 9th century at Strathfillan, Perthshire, Scotland, where there was an ancient monastery dedicated to him, which, like most of the religious houses of early times, was afterwards secularized.

Fillan is the patron saint of the mentally ill. In Strathfillan are the ruins of Saint Fillan's chapel, and hard by is the Holy Pool, in which the insane were, as late as the 19th century, bathed to obtain a cure by the saint's intercession.

Sir Walter Scott refers to it in '*Marmion*'.

He died in Strathfillan and was buried there, though his relics are reputed to have been used to inspire the Scots before the **Battle of Bannockburn.** To give thanks for his victory, Robert the Bruce later established **St Fillan's Priory**, of which just some ruins remain.

Artist J.P. Philip.

Robert the Bruce on the eve of Bannockburn receiving the sacrament from the Abbott of Inchaffray, St Fillan's arm bone, ***'The Mayne'*** was carried at front of his army as well as the Monymusk Reliquary containing a relic of St Columba.

Tour 4, Castles of the North East.

Nairn.

Nairn: The Castle is now long gone but is commemorated with this plaque and the naming of the square.

CASTLE SQUARE
NAIRN CASTLE WAS FIRST BUILT NEAR HERE ABOUT THE 12TH CENTURY, PROBABLY BY KING WILLIAM THE LION. DURING THE WARS OF INDEPENDENCE THE GOOD HOUSE OF NAIRN WAS OCCUPIED BY ENGLISH TROOPS, BUT RETAKEN BY SCOTS FORCES. IN 1583 JAMES VI INSTRUCTED JOHN CAMPBELL OF CAWDOR, CONSTABLE AND SHERIFF TO PERUSE THE DEMOLISHERS AND DOWNCASTERS WHO WERE STEALING THE STONES OF WHAT HAD BECOME A RUIN.

Auldearn.

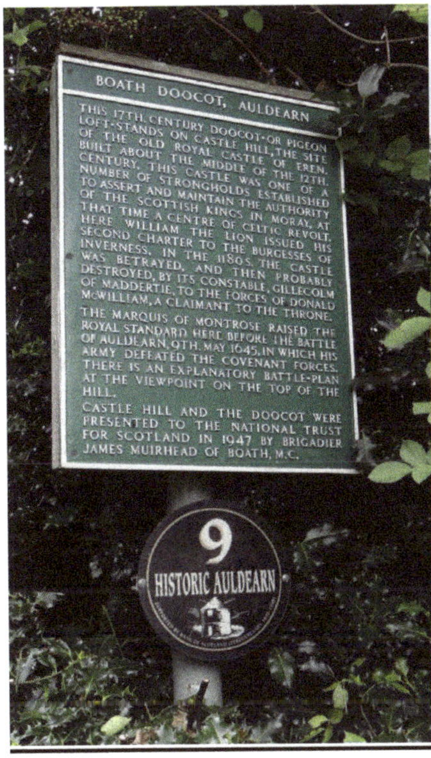

Nothing remains of the medieval Castle that once stood at Auldearn except the hill on which it once stood.

Nowadays the Boath Doocot sits atop the hill. Bruce took William II Earl of Ross to task here, making him sign a bond of loyalty.

This was an incredible act of restraint given that William had captured the Bruce womenfolk at St Duthac's Chapel in Tain and handed them over to Edward I.

Brodie Castle.

Bruce didn't attack a castle here; however a letter from him is on display here.
The original Z-plan tower house was completed in 1567 by Clan Brodie and was partially burned by fire in 1645 by Lewis Gordon of Clan Gordon, the 3rd Marquis of Huntly. In 1824, architect William Burn was commissioned to convert it into a mansion house in the Scots Baronial style, but these additions were only partially completed & were later remodelled by James Wylson (c. 1845).

It is widely accepted that the family has been associated with the land on which the castle stands since around 1160, when it is believed that King Malcolm IV gave the land to the family.

"...A 700-year-old letter written by Robert the Bruce has finally returned to Brodie Castle after three years away from display. Visitors to the National Trust for Scotland (NTS) property, between Forres and Nairn, will get to see the letter next month during their guided tour around the castle.

The centuries-old letter reveals that Robert the Bruce demanded that the Thane of Brodie take proper care of his millpond.

His neglect, the monarch makes clear, had annoyed the local monks of Pluscarden Abbey, near Elgin. The letter – written in 1312 in Latin on vellum paper – was removed from display at the property in 2019 after it started to fade due to light damage and humidity.

Members of the public, however, came to the aid of the NTS to help raise £5,231 through a crowdfunder to help the trust purchase a case to ensure it could return on display at Brodie Castle. The NTS team hope its return will help draw new and returning visitors to the castle after its finances suffered as a result of the pandemic restrictions.

NTS operations manager James Dean said he was delighted to see the Robert the Bruce letter back on display at Brodie Castle. Mr Dean said: "From the start of March when we fully reopen, visitors will see the Robert the Bruce letter on display in a new case.

"I'm so delighted about the letter returning and for new and returning visitors to see it. "The letter is certainly a major hook to draw people back to Brodie Castle."

It was previously hoped that the letter would return in July 2021.However, delays to the specialist case arriving derailed the plans. He added: "We are glad the letter is back after some delays.

"The last time it was on display to public was in September 2018. "We plan to switch the letter out halfway through the season to give it a rest from the light."

Forres Castle.

Forres, May blossom at the site of the medieval castle.

Surprisingly the castle was not located at the nearby Cluny Hill to the east of the town but at the western end of what is now the High Street, situated on the eastern bank of the Burn of Mosset.

Now a monument to an army surgeon marks the spot with no mention of the castle or its history.

Axe Medallion made from the Bruce Oak,
a temporary commemoration to Bruce's connection to the castle.

The castle of Forres was first mentioned in the reign of Alexander II, its mill was included in the foundation grant to Pluscarden Abbey in 1230.

The castle was taken from the English and burned to the ground by **Andrew Moray** in 1297. It remained in a ruinous state for half a century until it was rebuilt in stone by the Earls of Moray.

By 1488 the mansion called Castlehill at Forres was the principal building here, held by the **Dunbars of Westfield** who became hereditary Sheriffs, and appear to have built a tower house on the site.

The defences and tower had fallen into disrepair by the time the last Dunbar of Westfield died in 1711, and today the only indication that a castle stood here is the old sign on the park gates.

Elgin Castle.

Elgin castle was eventually sacked by Bruce and slighted after two previously unsuccessful attacks during Bruce's harrying of Buchan. The castle was repaired by Thomas Randolph, (d.1332), who was granted the earldom of Moray by his uncle, Bruce in the period 1312-14.

"...Elgin Castle must have once dominated the town almost as much as its justly renowned cathedral. Built on the summit of Lady Hill, the site permits a courtyard castle measuring 80 metres by 50 to fit comfortably on it. Around the northern, eastern and southern sides of the hill are the remains of a terrace which is reminiscent of earlier fortifications, and suggest that the castle site may have been defended since perhaps the 8th or 9th centuries.

The 16th and 17th century depictions of Elgin suggest that the main tower was at the end facing the town, but it was not a Norman-style keep, but something more modest, probably a type of hall-house. Elgin Castle was in existence by 1160, when it appears as a royal castle, and was probably founded by David I in association with the creation of Elgin as a royal burgh in that year.
The castle appears in records of the Crown down to the Wars of Independence, and was used by Edward I as a residence in 1296.

In 1303 it was burned by the Scots, and again in 1307. The castle was repaired by the Earls of Moray later in the 14th century and last appears in the records in 1390 as the Earl's Castle. It was probably sacked during the Douglas rebellion of the 1450s, after which the Dunbar Sheriffs used a residence in town, part of which survives as the Thunderton House public house..."

Left: The Bruce Oak Heart rests atop Elgin Map Plinth.
Right: Aerial view of the remains of Elgin Castle atop Lady Hill. (Canmore).

Duffus Castle, north of Elgin.

In about 1270 the castle and estates passed by marriage to Sir Reginald Cheyne. In the wars of independence between Scotland and England, Cheyne was a supporter of Edward I of England and held the castle for him. It was attacked and destroyed by the Scots led by Andrew Moray in 1297, during the campaign that culminated at the Battle of Stirling Bridge. It was again captured by Robert the Bruce in 1307. (Undiscovered Scotland).

Left: Stone road up to the castle tower.
Right: Looking down onto the defensive ditch. A classic Motte and Bailey construction.

Cullen Castle, (site of), & **Cullen Old Parish Church.**

Left: Hill site of Cullen Castle in the historic County of Banffshire,
overlooking the town and Moray Firth Coast.
Right: Cullen Old Parish Church.

Elizabeth de Burgh, the Ulster-born daughter of a nobleman and the 2nd wife of Bruce, was visiting the north-east town in 1327 when she died after falling from her horse.
While plans were made to transport her body to the traditional royal burial site at Dunfermline Abbey, the local people removed her internal organs so the body could survive the long arduous journey more appropriately

Her viscera, *'interiores partes'*, were removed and interred in Cullen Church ahead of her remains being taken south.

Bruce was filled with both grief at the loss of his wife and also with appreciation for the arrangements the townsfolk made and so he endowed a chaplainry here to pray for her soul and ordered for the church to receive money "for all eternity". The payment, originally five Scots pounds, was so that Elizabeth would be remembered in a special service every year. This memorial service has continued to be held every October, the month she died, when locals also pray for everyone lost in the community over the past 12 months.
Today the money equates to £2.10 a year with Moray Council now taking responsibility for paying as a symbolic gesture for the continuation of Bruce's instruction.

In memory of this story, additional Medallions made from the Bruce Oak were taken to Cullen, a **'Heart 'broken in two',** (as a poignant symbol), and a **Pilgrim's Cross**, both courtesy of Duncan Thomson of the Strathleven Artizans.

The medallions were placed on the alter and also on the pew where local tradition has her viscera interred.

On the return home to the Vale of Leven the medallions were then placed at St Serf's Chapel, Levengrove Park, where Bruce's own viscera were interred ahead of his burial in Dunfermline Abbey.

Banff Castle, (site of).

Plaque commemorating the medieval castle that once stood on the site of what is now a Georgian Building

Entrance Gate and Georgian Mansion, once the site of the medieval castle.

Left: Info board at Banff, picture of the original defensive wall on the top left hand side.
Right: Aerial View, Banff, Castle.

The remains of Banff Castle consist of part of a walled courtyard and substantial earthworks from a royal castle dating back to the 13th century or earlier.

Within the walls of the courtyard is an 18th century house bearing the same name.

The castle may have been founded by David I when that king established the royal borough of Banff, but the earliest mention of it in records is 1290, when it was given an English garrison during the Great Cause.

Although it changed hands several times, Banff was the last castle in English hands north of the Grampians by 1309.

Robert Bruce granted it to the Earl of Ross, and in 1396 Banff Castle and its associated estate passed to the carl of Buchan – whose successors retained it into the 17th century before selling it in 1636.

The house was then built c.1750, and the ruins of the old castle were eventually tidied up (i.e. largely removed) in 1815 – probably involving a certain amount of rebuilding of the curtain wall.

Today it is possible to walk around the outside of the house and within the grounds as it is held in public ownership. ***Banff Castle and Old Castle | Canmore***

Tour 5, Argyll.

Inverary Castle – Sir Neil Campbell.

Inverary Castle, Seat of Clan Campbell.

Left: Campbell Heraldic Panel, (St Conan's Kirk, Loch Awe).

Right, Bruce Oak Heart rests on the fireplace at Inverary Castle. Sir Neil Campbell was Bruce's Comrade-in-Arms and organised galleys at Dumbarton for Bruce in order for him to take flight to the Western Isles after the routs at Methven & Dalrigh.

Battle of Cruachan / The Pass of Brander.

Battle Cairn, Lochawe Train Station.

Plaque Reads:

In 1308, West of here and probably a little to the East of the falls of Cruachan, King Robert the Bruce won a decisive victory over John of Lorn, last remaining leader of the House of Comyn faction opposed to Bruce's Kingship. John of Lorn's forces held a strong position on the slopes of Cruachan, but were out- flanked from above by Highlanders and Borderers under Sir James Douglas. This victory enabled King Robert to unite Scots behind him against the English invader.

The Battle of the Pass of Brander, although just a small part of the Wars of Scottish Independence, was still a pivotal part of the Scots Civil War between the Bruce and Balliol factions. The MacDougalls of Argyll were kinsmen of **John Comyn**, also known as the **Red Comyn,** through marriage, and were thus allied with the **Balliol** faction. Bruce stood against the Balliols, and participated in the **killing of the Red Comyn on February 10th, 1306, before the high altar of the Greyfriars Church in Dumfries**.

This slaying was a decisive act in Scottish political history, for soon after the Bruce was crowned with the full support of the **Scottish Church**. Despite this, Bruce now faced formidable obstacles in the form of an internal Scottish struggle.

With the murder of John the Red Comyn, his extensive network of family and kinsmen agreed to fight on the side of the English against Bruce, who they considered to be the greater threat than the Overlordship of Edward I. The Balliol faction controlled large and strategically important lands throughout the realm; in **Galloway, Lochaber, Atholl, Ross, Buchan**, as well as **Badenoch & Strathspey**.

Much of Argyll was under the control of **Alexander MacDougall, The Lord of Lorne,** who had been related to the **Red Comyn** by marriage. Soon after the Bruce was defeated by the English at the Battle of **Methven,** what was left of his army was decimated by Alexander's son, **John of Lorne**, at the Battle of Dalrig. Bruce narrowly escaped capture and was forced into hiding.

Bruce recovered from these disasters and descended on Ayrshire in the spring of 1307 to begin a guerrilla campaign, fighting against both English military strength and Scots enemies.
Edward I died on the way north to begin his own campaign, leaving his less effective son **Edward II**, in control of the army. Edward II turned his attention to English domestic troubles instead, and left his Scottish allies to manage as best they could.

The Bruce's first attack came in **September of 1307 in Galloway**, *(the hereditary home of the Balliols),* against the **MacDowalls**, *(the powerful feudal family then known as the Macdougalls of Galloway),* and the **Macanns.** The fighting was believed to be so fierce that the local peasantry took refuge over the border in Cumberland and the leading men in Galloway appealed to Edward II for help, however this was in vain and they were forced to pay tribute to the Bruce in return for a truce.

Bruce then turned his attention to the north, breaking through the English-held Lowlands and heading for the **Red Comyn's old stronghold in Lochaber**. This march into the Highlands was supported by a fleet of galleys sailing up **Loch Linnhe.**

John 'The Lame', acting for his elderly father, asked for a truce, unable to face the full force of this combined attack. Bruce then went **north-east** to settle concerns with his principal enemy, the Red Comyn's cousin and namesake, **John Comyn, the 3rd Earl of Buchan**.

This campaign lasted through the winter season, with the climax taking part at the **Battle of Barra / aka Inverurie, in May of 1308**. Bruce was now at liberty to turn his full attention back to unfinished business in the west. **Alexander MacDougall**, John the Lame's father, too old and sick to take part in the fighting, lay in his castle at **Dunstaffnage** and his son John was left with preparing for the expected onslaught to come.

In the **summer of 1308,** John's army took up position in the narrow Pass of Brander, where the **River Awe** cuts through the southern slope of **Ben Cruachan** on its way down from **Loch Awe.**
John, who was recovering from an illness, observed his army's dispositions from a **galley** on Loch Awe. His men were hidden in the hillside, overlooking the narrow path through the pass.
A party of **Highlanders loyal to the Bruce, commanded by Sir James Douglas**, climbed even higher up the mountain and positioned themselves at Bruce's enemy's rear.

The slopes of Ben Cruachan, the Pass of Brander lie to the west on the narrowing shore of Loch Awe. The MacDougall's were caught in a vice on the slopes of Ben Cruachan, with Sir James Douglas behind them and Bruce in front of them.

As the **MacDougalls** attacked Bruce's force below them John's men caught in a trap, with Bruce and his men coming from below and the Good Sir James Douglas from above.
The men MacDougall men were eventually broken and chased westwards across the **River Awe** back to **Dunstaffnage -** while John lamely escaped down the loch in his galley, eventually taking refuge in England.

John's father **Alexander, The Lord of Argyll** surrendered and paid homage to Bruce, but left the following year to join his son in exile.

Loch Awe narrows at the Pass of Brander.

St Conan's Kirk, Lochawe.

Effigy of Robert the Bruce, commemorating the Battle of Cruachan / Pass of Brander.

Bottom: Left: Heraldic Panel to MacDougall of Lorn. Right: Detail of Bruce effigy.

The coming of the **Callander and Oban Railway** in the late 1870s opened up what had previously been the largely deserted north shore **of Loch Awe**. The island of **Innis Chonain**, close to the shore, was purchased by **Walter Campbell**, who then built a house there for himself, his sister and his mother.

The nearest church was at **Dalmally,** a long journey for the elderly Mrs Campbell. Walter Campbell therefore decided to build a church in a more convenient location for his mother and picked a site on the steep north shore of Loch Awe. **St Conan's Kirk** was born.

The original St Conan's Kirk was built between 1881 and 1886, and comprised the nave and part of the choir of the later church that visitors see today. Walter Campbell had grander plans, however, and in 1907 he began work on a much more ambitious church.Walter worked on this until his death in 1914, and his sister **Helen** ran the project from 1918 until her death in 1927. The church was completed by their trustees. All the stone used to build St Conan's came from boulders on nearby hillsides that were rolled to the site before being worked.

The new St Conan's Kirk was first used for worship in 1930. Walter Campbell did not design the church to conform to any particular style. Rather he took ideas and designs from different places and periods and produced something that serves as a collection of what he thought were interesting features drawn from many other churches. In the **Bruce Chapel** there is an effigy of Robert the Bruce, carved from wood with an alabaster face and hands. Below the effigy is a small chamber containing a bone of Robert the Bruce, brought from Dunfermline Abbey.

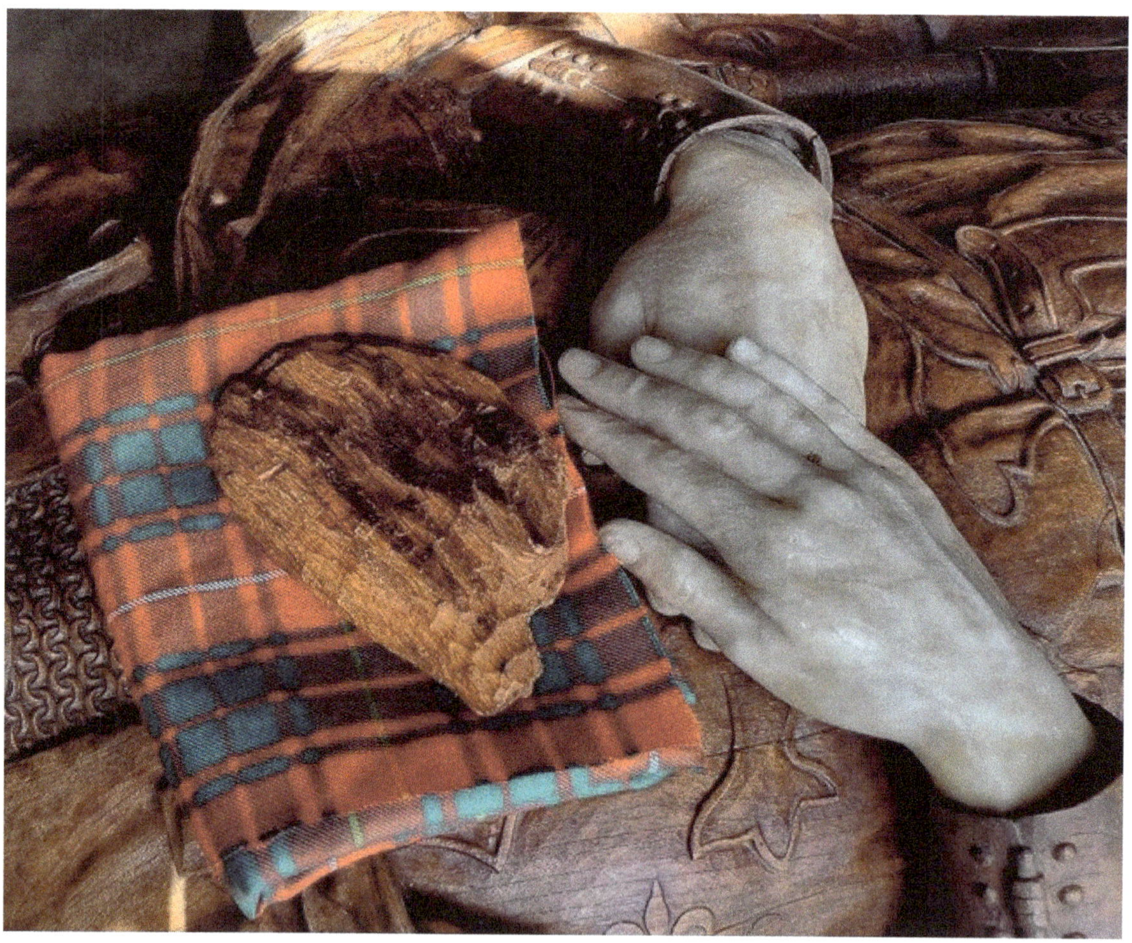

Dunnollie Castle, Oban.

There was a fortification on this high promontory since the Early Middle Ages at a time, when Dunollie was the royal centre of the ***Cenél Loairn*** within the kingdom of Dál Riata.

The Irish annals record that ***"Dun Ollaigh"*** was attacked three times, in 686, 698, and in 701.
It was subsequently rebuilt in 714 by **Selbach mac Ferchair** (died 730), the King of Dál Riata credited with destroying the site in 701. Excavations in the 1970s suggest that this early fortification was abandoned some time in the 10th century.
The area around Dunollie subsequently became part of the semi-independent **Kingdom of the Isles**, ruled over by **Somerled** in the 12th century. On his death the **MacDougalls** became Lords of Lorne. **Dougall**, Somerled's son, held most of Argyll and also the islands of **Mull, Lismore, Jura, Tiree, Coll** and many others in the 12th century.

Excavations show that Dunollie was refortified with an earthwork castle in either the late 12th or 13th century. The builder may have been Dougall, or his son **Duncan.**

Ewan MacDougall, great-grandson of Somerled and the third chief of the MacDougalls, switched the clan's allegiance in the mid 13th century: initially allied with **Haakon IV** of Norway, from the 1250s Ewan remained loyal to the **Kings of Scotland.**

In the 14th century Ewan's grandson, and the son of Alexander, **John MacDougall**, (known as ***John of Lorne*** *or* ***Iain 'Bacach' John the Lame***), along with his kinsmen the **Comyns,** sided with the **Balliols** against the ambitions of **Robert the Bruce.**

John's army defeated the Bruce at the **Battle of Dalrigh in 1306**, but Bruce returned and crushed the MacDougalls at the **Battle of the Pass of Brander in 1308**.

The MacDougall lands of Lorne were subsequently forfeit and were given to the **Campbells**, however Dunollie, and other estates, were regained later in the 14th century.
The existing castle ruins date largely from the 15th century.

Dunstaffnage Castle, Dunbeg, Argyll.

Set on top of a rocky outcrop three miles north of Oban, Dunstaffnage Castle is a striking fortification standing sentinel over what was once the most important junction on the sea-lanes off the west coast of Scotland. The strategic location means that this has been a defended site for nearly 1,500 years.

In the 600s the **Kings of Dalriada,** (the Kingdom of the Scots) who migrated to Argyll from Ireland, built a stronghold here and it has been suggested that this was the original keeping place of the Stone of Destiny. By 1249 the fortress here was held by the Macdougalls, appointed by **King Håkon IV of Norway.** In July 1249 Dunstaffnage was to be the first target of **King Alexander II** in his campaign to seize the Hebrides from Norwegian rule. However, with his fleet assembled in **Oban Bay**, Alexander died in unexplained circumstances on the Isle of **Kerrera.**

Oban Bay, the **Isle of Kerrera** just offshore and the mountains on Mull in the background, from McCaig's Folly, Oban.

Dunstaffnage Castle and the Macdougalls lived to fight another day: a day that came almost 60 years later at the **Battle of the Pass of Brander.**
Much of the castle visible today was built by the **Macdougalls** in the 1200s.

It is not known whether it was this castle or its predecessor on the site that was Alexander's target in 1249. The castle did, however, transfer to royal possession when it was captured after a siege by Robert the Bruce in 1309.

The Chiefs of **Clan MacArthur** were subsequently appointed as hereditary **Captains of Dunstaffnage Castle**, and it remained in their hands until **1470,** when custody was transferred to the **1st Earl of Argyll, Colin Campbell**.

In **1502** the castle was passed from the Earl to his cousin, whose family still hold the title of hereditary Captain.

Oban – and it's 'Highland Cathedral'.

Bruce Oak Heart at the Highland Cathedral, St Columba's.

RC Diocese of Argyll & The Isles.

Ardchattan Priory, North Connel.

In 1308, Robert the Bruce's campaign in the area included holding a council of local chiefs at the Priory, which is believed to have been the **last Gaelic-speaking parliament in Scotland.**
According to accounts, the **Yew Trees** at Ardchattan were inspected by Bruce and cut to make at least some of the longbows used at the **Battle of Bannockburn**

The Priory was established around 1230 by an obscure order of monks, the **Valliscaulians** from France. They followed a strict form of monastic rule, with emphasis more on the 'ascetic religious life' rather than on manual work.

Left: Priory window view onto Ben Cruachan – easy to imagine Bruce looking onto the site of his victory against the MacDougalls. Right: Ancient grave slab.

Left: Grave markers. Right: Claymore depicted in C14th/15th stone.

Houses were limited to no more than 20 brothers, and the monks' livelihood depended on rents and teinds (tithes) from endowments. Their church, in common with all Valliscaulian houses, was dedicated to **St Mary the Virgin** and **St John the Baptist.**

The original 13th century priory was rebuilt in the 15th century, when the monks' Choir was extended and a new refectory (dining hall) constructed. Monastic life eventually came to an end with the Protestant Reformation of 1560. The buildings and endowments were appropriated by John Campbell, later bishop of the Isles, and have remained with the **Clan Campbell** ever since.

The priory was founded by **Duncan MacDougall**, Lord of Lorne and builder of **Dunstaffnage Castle** near Oban. At this time kings of Scotland and Norway were fighting for control of Argyll and the Inner Hebrides. Duncan may have invited the Valliscaulians to Ardchattan to ingratiate himself with the Scottish king, **Alexander II.**

Alexander had recently established a monastery for this obscure order at **Pluscarden, near Elgin**. The Valliscaulians, whose mother house was in the Val des Choux in Burgundy, only ever set up daughter houses outside France in Germany and Scotland.

The third Valliscaulian house in Scotland was **Beauly,** west of Inverness, founded by the Bisset family.
The priory was dominated by the **MacDougalls** throughout most of its existence. By the end of the 15th century, the position of prior was monopolised by the family.

But in **1506** the last MacDougall prior, **Eugenius** (Eogan), was deposed. The new prior, **Duncan MacArthur**, attempted in vain to revive the zeal of the founding brethren. In **1538** there were just six monks in residence, and by the Reformation in 1560 a mere three.

In **1602**, Archibald Campbell, son of Bishop John Campbell, began the process of converting the old priory into a private house. While the church remained in use as the parish kirk until 1732, the monks' cloister was converted into a house. The old refectory is still the family dining room.

Among the numerous fine grave markers and carved stones on display is the **MacDougall Cross:**

- Commissioned by **Prior Eugenius MacDougall** in 1500, it was carved by **John Ó Brolchán,** a stone-carver from Iona.
- It is one of the few examples of West Highland carving recording the sculptor's name.
- The cross bears a **Crucifixion** scene on one side and an image of the **Virgin and Child** on the other. **References: Historic Environment Scotland**

MacDougall Cross.

Tour 6, Central Scotland & Borders.

Lanark - Bruce Oak Heart taken to town's mural commemorating William Wallace.

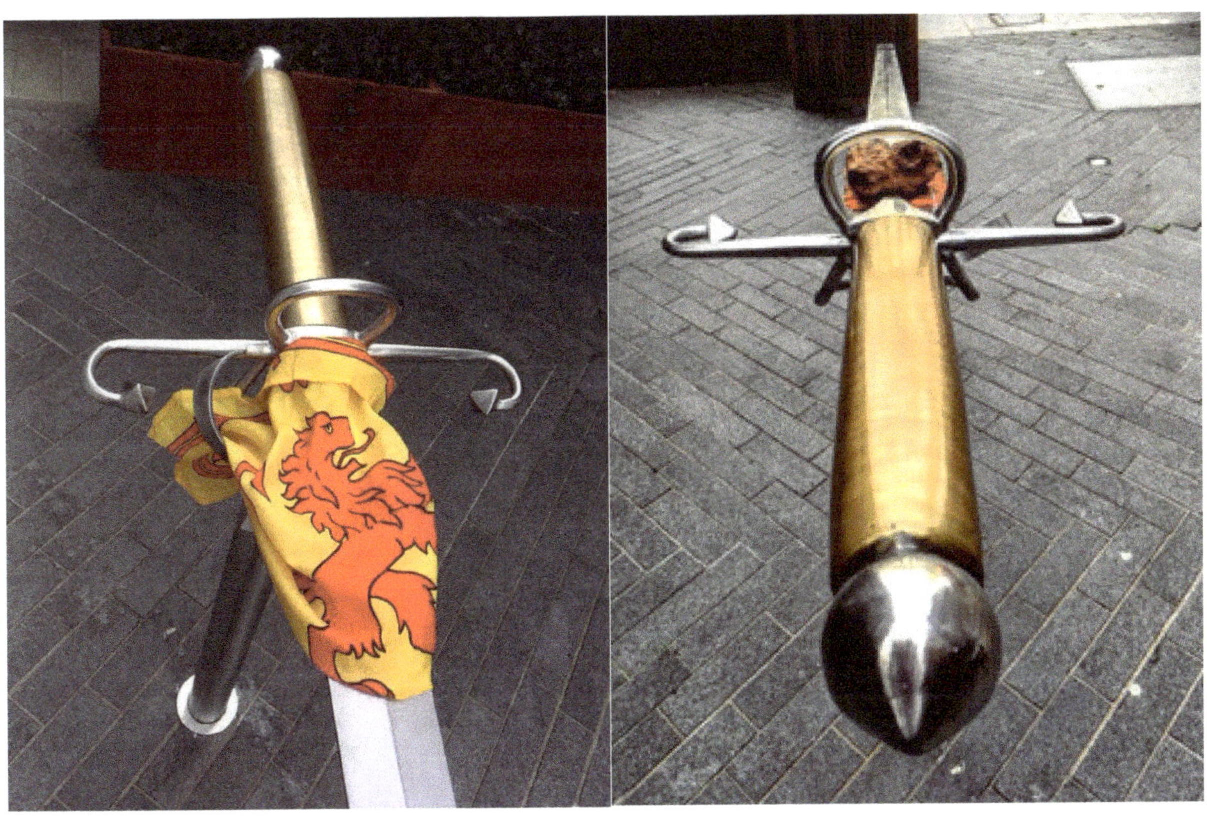

Bruce Oak Heart taken to a site of another Scots Patriot, William Wallace.

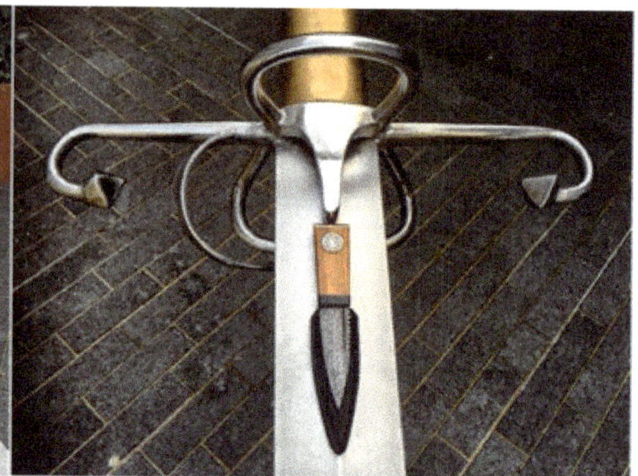

WALLACEHOUSE

Sir William Wallace

Peebles Hydro Hotel, Scottish Borders.

The Bannockburn Room.
On 22 July 1298, Wallace was defeated by the English at the Battle of Falkirk. **John Comyn** may have been present at the battle, possibly among the Scottish cavalry who deserted from the field of battle. William Wallace later resigned the Guardianship of Scotland and Comyn and Robert the Bruce was appointed in his place.

The traditional enmity between the Bruces and Comyn families still burned fiercely and at a meeting in Peebles in **August 1299** an argument erupted, during which Comyn was reported to have seized the Bruce by the throat.

A chronicler relates Comyn "leapt on Robert Bruce, Earl of Carrick, and took him by the throat," and that Comyn's uncle, John, Earl of Buchan leapt on **William Lamberton, Bishop of St. Andrews**, "and they held them fast until the **Steward** and others went and stopped the scuffle." William Lamberton, Bishop of St Andrews, was appointed as a third Guardian in 1299 to act as mediator.

Peebles Hydro Hotel & view onto the Border Hills.

Left: Yellow and Black Standard of Sir Neil Campbell.
Right: English Calvary in disarray.

In the **Bannockburn Room** of the Peebles Hydro Hotel is almost a third of the original panorama '***The Battle of Bannockburn'*** by German painter **Ernst Philipp Fleischer** (1850 - 1930) who painted several war panoramas.

In 1887 he travelled to Scotland for field studies of the battlefield.

His painting of the battle enjoyed considerable success in Glasgow in 1888 where it was exhibited at the panorama rotunda in Sauchiehall Street.

Scottish hotelier Albert M. Theim, purchased several of Fleischer's panoramas.

Large segments of the original panoramas of 'The Battle of Bannockburn' and 'The Battle of Omdurman' are today pasted to walls in the hotel.

Bannockburn battle scenes,
German painter Ernst Philipp Fleischer

Yellow and Red Standard of Thomas Randolph, Earl of Moray.

Melrose Abbey.

The centuries old Bruce Oak, rough hewn into the symbolic shape of Bruce's Heart,
finally joins the real 'Braveheart' buried at Melrose Abbey after being recovered after the Battle of Teba and returned to Scotland – together with a rock from Teba itself and other tokens made from the Bruce Oak.

'Home is where the Heart is'.
Stone from Teba, Bruce Oak Heart Medallions and Sgian.

Melrose Abbey & Eildon Hills

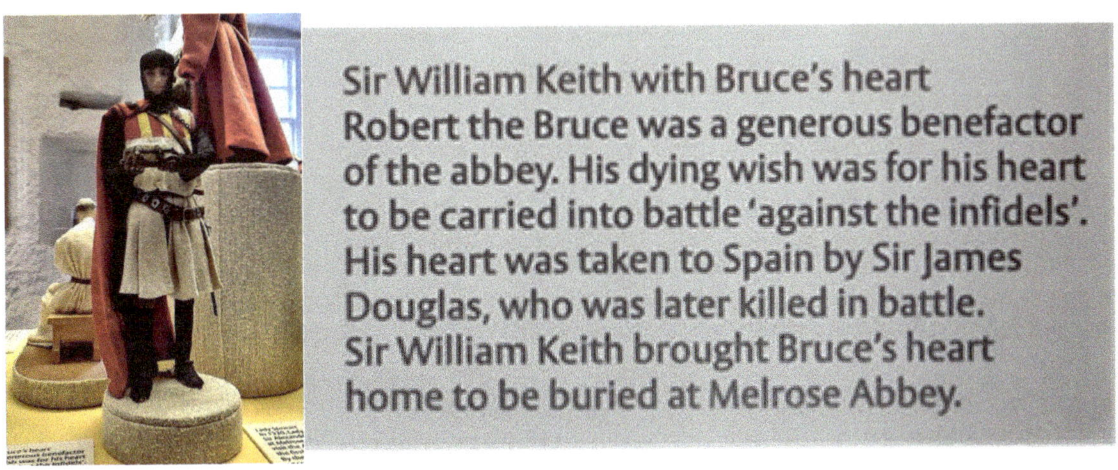

Model of Sir William Keith carrying the Heart of Bruce, Melrose Abbey Museum.

Galashiels.

Town Mural with flag comprising Lion Rampant and Douglas Heraldry.

Left: National Tapestry of Scotland, Galashiels.

Right: Image of The Battle of Bannockburn from the Tapestry.

Abbotsford, near Galashiels, home of Sir Walter Scott.

Scott was an avid collector of military and other memorabilia. He obtained a copy of the cast of Bruce's skull and wrote ***The Lord Of The Isles*** mentioning Bruce.

Left: Abbotsford: Right: Cast of Robert the Bruce's skull, left of mantelpiece.

Bruce Oak Heart & Cast of the King's Skull.

Left: Sir Walter Scott's writing desk and chair.

Right: Chair made of reclaimed wood from the house at Robroyston where William Wallace was captured

Selkirk.

Lochcarron of Scotland Mill.

A request to see a ream of Bruce Tartan brought out to place the Heart on was duly obliged.

Kirk o' The Forest – Bruce and Wallace, Guardians of Scotland.

This ‘auld church’, built in 1747, is thought to be at least the third church on the site.

It is widely believed to be the *Kirk o' the Forest* where Robert Bruce and the rest of the Scottish nobility gathered in the aftermath of the Battle of Stirling Bridge in 1297.

The purpose of that meeting was to create William Wallace a knight of the realm, Guardian and Protector of Scotland. The church was falling in to decay by the mid-1800s when a new church was built in the town.

The town of Selkirk said to come from Old English ***'scheleschirche'*** meaning church in the woods.

Medallions representing Bruce and Wallace available from the Society of William Wallace.

Hawick.

'Turning of the Bull' Monument, origins of the Turnbull name connected to Robert the Bruce.

"King Robert the Bruce went hunting in the great wood of Caledon near Stirling and narrowly escaped with his own life when one of the great white bulls rushed fiercely at him. Then a man of great spirit leapt before the King and, grappling with the bull, cast it to the earth with great force and held it there while the remaining hunters slew it with their weapons. Thereafter, William Rule, the Borders man who rescued the King was called Turn-e-bull. Hector Boece, Historian,1526"

Tour 7, Scone Palace, Moot Hill & Perth.

Members of the Strathleven Artizans take the Bruce Oak Heart to Scone

and to the replica of the Stone of Destiny at Moot Hill.

Chronicle of Walter of Guisborough, ed. H. Rothwell, Camden Society, 1957:

Translated by J. Russell,

Bruce had himself crowned King of Scotland and went into open rebellion against the ailing Edward I. Some of his strongest and bravest supporters were women, such as Christiana, Lady of the Isles, who supplied him with galleys and troops, and the more famous Isabel, Countess of Buchan, who stole away from her pro-English husband in order to crown him.

Isabel and the women of Bruce's family suffered terrible fates when they were captured by Edward's forces. He ordered the most active of the women to be confined in wooden cages on the tops of towers, exposed to the elements with only a little privy to which to retreat, yet their fate was better than that of the men who fell into his hands and whom he ordered to be hung, drawn and quartered.

Here is Walter of Guisborough's account of Bruce's coronation and what followed.

At the beginning of AD 1306, the aforesaid Robert de Bruce, on the day of the Annunciation to the Blessed Mary, had himself crowned as King of Scotland at Scone, in the presence and with the agreement of four bishops, five earls and the people of the land.

And the wife of the Earl of Buchan, who was the daughter of the Earl of Fife, to whom by hereditary right it belonged to place the crown on the head of the new king, secretly withdrew from her lord, bringing her lord's war-horses which he had sent home, so that she might exercise that office. This angered her lord, who had stood forth in loyalty to the King of England, and since she had been captured in the same year, he wished to kill her, but the King forbade him and ordered her to be placed upon the wall [the top of a tower] of the castle of Berwick, secured in a wooden cage, so that she could be seen and recognised by those passing by.

And she remained many days, thus enclosed and on a strict regimen. And the King sent two bishops, namely those of Glasgow and St Andrews in Scotland, together with the Abbot of Scone, since they had been captured the same year, into England to different castles and they remained closely confined until the death of the King. And so once he had heard and learnt of the coronation of the new king, the lord the King of England, on the feast of Pentecost, sent forward with an armed band, some of his soldiers, namely the Lord Henry de Percy, the Lord Aylmer de Valence and the Lord Robert Clifford to oppose the new king and hunt him down . . .

And the new king fled and they pursued him as far as the isle of Kintyre, and they besieged the castle of that place, believing that he had withdrawn into the same place, but he had gone away into the furthest isles of that region.

And when the castle had been taken by storm, they found one of the new king's brothers, namely the Lord Neil de Bruce, with the new queen and many others. Taking them with them as far as Berwick in the presence there of the justices of the Lord, the King of England, who by the King's command had assembled in that place, the men were judicially condemned, hanged, drawn and beheaded.

And because the new queen was a daughter of the Earl of Ulster, he at the beginning of the war waged by his son-in-law, the Lord Robert de Bruce (lest the lord the King of England should suspect him of any evil against him), sent his two sons to the King to be held fast at the King's good will to excuse himself because he had always shown himself loyal to him. Also on account of one word which she had said to her husband when at his coronation he was speaking to her and said, 'Rejoice now, my wife, because you have been made a Queen and I a King,' she is said to have replied to him, 'I am afraid my Lord that we have been made King and Queen, as boys are made in summer games.'

Therefore for those two causes the King sent her with her household to stay at her manor of Brustewych and ordered her to be maintained with honour. [As to] the earl of Atholl, who had fled from that castle and after some interval had been captured, although the Queen of England and many nobles asked the King on his behalf for his life, especially because he was a near relative to the lord the King of England, the King ordered that he should be brought to London and hanged higher than the rest. And because he who had been a prominent blood relation was found to be a traitor, the King ordered him to be beheaded and burned after his hanging, which was done.

As to Christopher Seton, who had married the new king's sister, Mary [in fact Christian] by name, although he was English, when he was taken in the castle of Lochdore [Lochdoon Castle] and afterwards his wife and many others, the King ordered that he be taken to Dumfries, where he had killed a soldier, and there to be drawn, hanged and beheaded. His two brothers and others who all agreed to and were present at the death of the lord John Comyn had a similar sentence and this from the King's special command. However, the King placed Christopher's wife in the monastery of Thyxsel, in Lindesay [Sixhills, Lincolnshire], and he placed the new king's daughter in the monastery of Watthon [Watton, Yorkshire].

Perth Museum, St John's Place. The stone purporting to be the Stone of Destiny is on display here – photography is strictly not allowed, (The Bruce Oak Heart came tantalisingly close).

Bruce's attack on Perth Castle.

March 15th 1312.

After the defeat of Wallace at the battle of Falkirk in 1298, Edward I had control over most of the large towns in Scotland.

The town of Perth was occupied, fortified and garrisoned with a large force of English soldiers. It was an important enough location to be the residence of Edward's son, Edward, Prince of Wales, for several years - however Edward I died in 1307 and Bruce had started the long battle to regain Scotland's independence.

In 1311, he and his followers besieged the town of Perth but were unable to breach the defences. In the spring of the following year another attempt was made.

"Bruce would not desist from his purpose, or suffer this single walled town for ever to baffle his efforts. Providing himself with scaling ladders, and such other instruments that he could find, he speedily renewed the siege, at a time when those within the town were pleasing themselves with the persuasion that they were enclosed within impregnable walls and had no future siege to fear. He chose a dark night and, in its silence taking a chosen band, conducted them himself in person, partly wading, partly swimming across a ditch deep broad and full of water that surrounded the walls.

The rest were animated on this, as on many other occasions, by the example of the daring valour with which the King exposed himself the foremost to danger.

The contest among them was who should first cross the ditch, and, by the scaling ladders which they had carried with them, mount the walls. This gallant and perilous enterprise succeeded.

The King himself was second to enter the town. The garrison and townspeople were easily overpowered. In the castle, and in the stores of the merchants, a considerable booty was found of those things which the captors wanted the most for the relief of their own necessities.

The slaughter of the vanquished was humanely stayed as soon as the resistance ceased. The houses were burned and the walls and fortifications levelled with the ground. By this happy achievement all Perthshire and Strathearn was freed from servitude to the English and reduced under the authority of King Robert."

Soon afterwards the castles of Roxburgh, Dumfries and Edinburgh fell to the Scottish forces.

Perthshire Diary.

Perth Concert Hall, Mill Street.

This was original site of Perth Castle, the hill on which it would once have stood now levelled.

Artist's impression of the original site of Perth Castle,
this plaque found on flood defence wall on the North Inch area of the town.

Left: Despite a plaque in **North Port** giving the date of the destruction of the Castle by flooding as 1210 AD, the 1911 edition of Encyclopaedia Britannica states that the castle was still in existence during the Wars of Independence in the 14th century. In the encyclopaedia, Bruce is stated to have attempted to destroy the castle to prevent its use by English armies.

Right: Plaque reads: **Portion of Old City Wall.**

On the north side of the narrow passageway that runs from Skinnergate to George Street a simple plaque indicates what is reputed to be the remains of the old city wall. There is debate however on whether this claim is justified. In the 19th century, plaques were sometimes put up based on less information than we would accept to-day.

This is undoubtedly an old wall and may rest on the foundations of an even earlier wall which along with the mill lade, (waterway), walls provided Perth's main defence. According to Thomas Hay Marshall the city walls were re-built by Edward.

Red Brig area of Perth and the Mill Lade Waterway which formed part of the defence around the town of Perth that Bruce and his army would have had to overcome.

Left: The Mill Lade, following the line of the original medieval waterway from a different angle,
Right: Modern day flood defences in the event the Mill Lade Floods.
Right: The Mill Lade Waterway lies behind this portion of medieval wall between Skinnergate & George St.

Left: View of Old City Wall. Right: Bruce Oak Axe Medallion – the town's defences are once more 'assailed'.

Tour 8, Aberdeen & East Coast.

Left: Bruce Oak Heart, and other Wood Craft, Trinity Shopping Centre, Aberdeen.
Right: 'Gie Dreich', a pewter sky over a granite city. Market Cross, Castle Street.

Left: High rise flats, Marischal Court, original location of Aberdeen Castle.

Right: Monument to the Gordon Highlanders. The Clan were present at Bannockburn.

The Bruce Oak Heart placed on the soldiers webbing – 'once more carried into battle'.

The modern day 'Patagonia Court' in Aberdeen. Local tradition has Bruce chasing the English Garrison in the castle down what was once the slope of a hill.

Left: Holding aloft the Bruce Oak Heart at Aberdeen's monument to Bruce.
He himself is holding aloft the Stocket Charter.

Right: Hazlehead Park, Aberdeen – *Bruce Freedom Lands*.

Aberdeen: The Freedom Lands.

In 1319, when the Kingdom of Scotland was passing through a period of depression and the victorious King Robert the Bruce felt he had an honourable duty to perform to those who helped him establish the independence of the Kingdom, a regular feudal Charter of the burgh of Aberdeen and of the Stocket forest was granted the burgesses. The Forest of the Stocket, together with certain additional areas, comprises what is known as "The Freedom Lands".

The Marches. The observance of boundaries or marches and the preservation of landmarks are of remote origin, and go back to the time when man took one of his early steps along the path of civilization. At first, no doubt, the landmarks were natural objects, such as hills, trees and streams, and the rough tracks or highways of the time, but as early society grew in complexity, the necessity for marks of artificial construction arose, and with these came the collateral necessity of guarding against their removal. A riding of the Marches at frequent intervals was undertaken for the purpose of ensuring that the landmarks were not moved, or if moved, that they were restored to their original position.

Cairn commemorating the Battle of Bannockburn 1314.

Right: Bruce presenting the Freedom Lands to the citizens of Aberdeen.

Cairn to the The Hership, (Harrying), of Buchan.

Bruce is associated with many caves, in Scotland & off the Irish Coast on Rathlin Island

Spider Tree Carving & Lion's Head Water Fountain - both with Bruce Oak Axe Medallion.

John Barbour and St Machar's Cathedral.

Left: Plaque to John Barbour, 53 Castle Street, Aberdeen. Right: St Machar's Cathedral.

John Barbour (c.1320 – 13 March 1395) was the first major named literary figure to write in Scots. His principal surviving work is the historical verse romance, **The Brus** (The Bruce).

Barbour was latterly Archdeacon of the Diocese of Aberdeen in Scotland. He also studied in Oxford and Paris.

Although he was a man of the church, his surviving writing is strongly secular in both tone and themes. His principal patron was Robert II and evidence of his promotion and movements before Robert Stewart came to power as king tend to suggest that Barbour acted politically on the future king's behalf.

Left: Wood Panel representing John Barbour.
Right: Barbour is thought to be buried under these flagstones.

Left: Robert the Bruce ahead of his army.
Right: Brig o' Balgownie over the River Don, Bruce funded the completion of its restoration.

Bruce Oak Heart at St Machar's Altar.

St Machar's Altar and Heraldry Panels on ceiling.

Right: The single arched Brig o' Balgownie upstream, and the modern day multi arched bridge over the River Don, represented in a stained glass window.

Local legend suggests that construction of the Brig O' Balgownie was started by **Henry Cheyne, Bishop of Aberdeen** in the late 13th or early 14th century and was completed by Robert the Bruce in thanks for the support from the townspeople.

The Brig O' Balgownie spans the River Don.

Old Meldrum – Battle of Barra.

From Historic Environment Scotland: **Inventory Battlefield, Battle of Barra:**

The Comyn's had been Bruce's most notable Scottish adversary up to this point, and with the destruction of their power base, both in the battle and the subsequent ravaging of Comyn lands in Buchan, they were no longer able to resist the King.

With their demise, Bruce was able to turn his full attention to English garrisons, embarking upon his 'scorched earth' campaign against their castles and leading to the Battle of Bannockburn in 1314. Barra thus marks the end of one phase of Bruce's military and royal career, and the beginning of the next.

The Battle of Barra was one of the many battles fought by Robert the Bruce in the period between his inauguration in 1306 and the Battle of Bannockburn in 1314. With the English distracted by events at home, Bruce turned to securing Scotland under his rule. At Barra, the King engaged an army led by John Comyn outside Inverurie and the battle quickly turned into a rout, with much of Comyn's army captured or slaughtered as they ran.

The relocated stone where Bruce is reputed to have rested after the Battle of Barra.

Left: Barra Castle, about two miles south of Oldmeldrum, Aberdeenshire, is adjacent to the site of the Battle of Barra / Inverurie which took place in 1308 where Bruce defeated John Comyn, Earl of Buchan. A castle has been on this site from the mid-13th century and was the seat of the King family. The current castle is an L-plan tower house dating from the early 16th century.

Right: From the castle, looking up to Barra Hill, the original site for 'Bruce's Seat'.

Dunnotar Castle, Near Stonehaven, Kincardineshire.

Dunnottar Castle: Dùn Fhoithear, ("fort on the shelving slope") is a ruined medieval fortress located upon a rocky headland on the north-eastern coast of Scotland, about 2 miles south of Stonehaven. The surviving buildings are largely of the 15th and 16th centuries, but the site is believed to have been fortified in the Early Middle Ages.

Dunnottar has played a prominent role in the history of Scotland through to the 18th-century Jacobite risings because of its strategic location and defensive strength.

In 1297 a Scottish force under **William Wallace** captured the castle. The English garrison inside take refuge in the church, but Wallace burns the church with the soldiers locked inside, and destroys the castle.

Clan Keith: The surname is derived from a number of placenames in Scotland which in turn were from the Brittonic word "coed" meaning "wood".

The name appears in a number of locations in Scotland, the earliest being a Norman adventurer, Hervey Keith who married an heiress of the warrior Marbhachair. Hervey was granted the lands of "Keth" from King David I around 1150. His son became Marischal (in charge of the horses) of the King of Scots.

Sir Robert de Keith led the Scots cavalry at the Battle of Bannockburn in 1314, (but died later at the Battle of Durham in 1346). His nephew was **William Keith of Galston** who returned Bruce's heart to Melrose Abbey after the death of the Sir James Douglas at the Battle of Teba in Andalucia.

The Keiths were made Hereditary Great Marischal by Bruce in a charter of 1324, a rank they held until 1715.

Sir Robert Keith, the Marishchal, escorted the young **David II** of Scotland when he fled to France to escape the usurpation Edward Balliol.

As leaders of the Scots cavalry, the Keiths were involved in most of the major battles over the centuries. **Lord Keith** survived the slaughter of the Battle of Flodden in 1513 and his standard from that battle has survived to this day.

While the Keiths were associated with Dunnotar a marriage to the heiress of Ackergill resulted in a move to Caithness, where they became involved in a long and bloody feud with the clan Gunn.

Dunnottar is also known as the place where the Honours of Scotland, the Scottish crown jewels, were hidden from Oliver Cromwell's invading army in the 17th century.

Fordoun, Aberdeenshire.

John of Fordun, (Fordoun), was probably a chaplain at St Machar's Cathedral in Aberdeen, and it is believed that he developed an interest in history in order to record Scotland's place in history and its wider links: all against the background of the tremendous destruction caused by the Wars of Independence against England. He was, in effect, an early Scottish nationalist.

Stracathro, Angus.

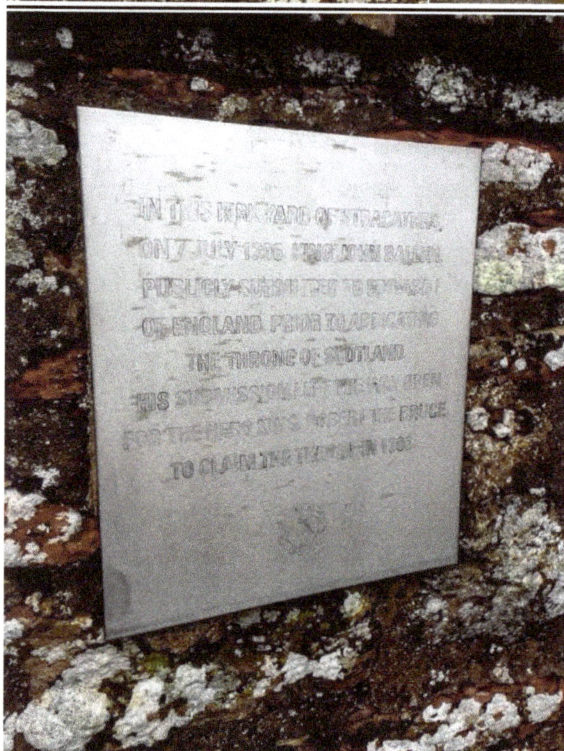

''In this Kirk Yard of Stracathro on 7 July 1296 King John Balliol publically submitted to Edward I of England prior to abdicating the throne of Scotland. His submission left the way open for the Hero King Robert The Bruce to claim the throne in 1306''

Plaque at Stracathro.

The crown of Scotland was awarded to John Balliol at Berwick on 17 November 1292. He swore fealty to Edward I and was installed as King at Scone and on 26 December at Newcastle upon Tyne, Northumberland, and did homage to Edward I for the Kingdom of Scotland. Edward soon made it clear that he regarded the country as his 'vassal state'. Balliol did not have the strength of character to resist, and the Scots resented Edward's demands.

When in 1294 Edward instructed them to supply soldiers for his war with France, they set up a council of ecclesiastics and noblemen to rule instead of Balliol - although 'in his name'. They then made a defensive alliance with **Philip IV of France** against England. This Treaty marked the formal beginning of the ***'Auld Alliance'*** between Scotland and France which was to last for nearly 300 years. Balliol finally renounced his fealty to Edward I on 5 April 1296.

Edward I marched north, defeated the Scots at the **Battle of Dunbar** in East Lothian and captured the castles of Roxburgh, Edinburgh and Stirling. The **Battle of Dunbar** was the only significant field action in the campaign of 1296. Edward I had invaded Scotland in 1296 to punish King John Balliol for his refusal to support English military action in France.

After the sack of Berwick-upon-Tweed, Edward rushed to complete the conquest of Scotland, remained in the town for a month, supervising the strengthening of its defences.

On 5 April, he received a message from King John renouncing his homage, to which he remarked,

"O' foolish knave! What folly he commits. If he will not come to us we will go to him."

The next objective in the campaign was the Earl of March's castle at Dunbar, a few miles up the coast from Berwick. March was on the side of the English, but his wife, **Marjory Comyn**, sister of the **Earl of Buchan,** did not share her husband's political loyalties and allowed her fellow Scots to occupy the castle.

Edward sent one of his chief lieutenants, **John de Warenne, 6th Earl of Surrey**, John Balliol's own father-in-law, northwards with a strong force of knights to invest the stronghold.

The defenders sent messages to King John, bivouacked with the main body of his army at nearby **Haddington**, asking for urgent assistance.

In response the army, or a large part of it, advanced to the rescue of Dunbar.

John, who was showing even less skill as a commander than he had as a king, did not accompany it. The campaign of 1296 was now to enter its final phase.

There is little evidence to suggest that Dunbar was anything other than an action between two bodies of mounted men-at-arms (armoured cavalry).

Surrey's force seems to have comprised one formation (out of four) of the English cavalry; the Scots force lead in part by Comyns probably represented the greater part of their cavalry element.

The two forces came in sight of each other on **27 April**. The Scots occupied a strong position on some high ground to the west.

To meet them, Surrey's cavalry had to cross a gully intersected by the **Spot Burn**.

As they did so their ranks broke up, and the Scots, deluded into thinking the English were leaving the field, abandoned their position in a disorderly downhill charge, only to find that Surrey's forces had reformed on **Spottsmuir** and were advancing in perfect order.

The English routed the disorganised Scots in a single charge. The action was brief and probably not very bloody, since the only casualty of any note was a minor Lothian knight, **Sir Patrick Graham,** though about 100 Scottish lords, knights and men-at-arms were taken prisoner.

According to one English source over ten thousand Scots died at the battle of Dunbar, however this is probably a confusion with the casualties incurred at the storming of Berwick.

The survivors fled westwards to the safety of **Selkirk Forest.** The following day Edward I appeared in person and Dunbar castle surrendered.

Some important prisoners were taken: **John Comyn, Earl of Buchan**, and the earls of **Atholl, Ross and Menteith**, together with 130 knights and esquires. All were sent into captivity in England.

The battle of Dunbar effectively ended the war of 1296. The remainder of the campaign was little more than a grand mopping-up operation. **James, the hereditary High Steward of Scotland,** surrendered the important fortress at **Roxburgh** without attempting a defence, and others were quick to follow his example.

Only **Edinburgh Castle** held out for a week against Edward's siege engines. A Scottish garrison sent out to help King John, who had fled north to Forfar, were told to provide for their own safety.

Edward himself, true to his word, advanced into central and northern Scotland in pursuit of King John. **Stirling Castle**, which guarded the vital passage across the River Forth was deserted save for a janitor who stayed behind to hand the keys to the English.

John reached **Perth on 21 June**, where he received messages from Edward asking for peace. Balliol, in surrendering, submitted himself to a protracted abasement. At Kincardine Castle on 2 July he confessed to rebellion and prayed for forgiveness. Five days later in the kirkyard of Stracathro he abandoned the treaty with the French.

On **7 July**, in the churchyard at **Stracathro** in Angus, Balliol surrendered himself to **Antony Beck, Bishop of Durham**. He was forced to seal a document confessing that he had wrongly allied himself with his overlord's enemies

The final humiliation came at Montrose on 8 July. Dressed for the occasion John was ceremoniously stripped of the vestments of royalty. Antony Bek, the Bishop of Durham, ripped the red and gold arms of Scotland from his surcoat, thus bequeathing to history the nickname Toom Tabard (empty coat) by which John has been known to generations of Scottish schoolchildren.

He and his son Edward were sent south into captivity. Soon after, the English king followed, carrying in his train the Stone of Scone and other relics of Scottish nationhood. Balliol's ceremonial disrobing has been described as one of the saddest hours in Scottish history. The current church at Stracathro was built in 1799 on the site of the medieval church, which, by 1792, was described as ruinous.

Arbroath Abbey, Abbey Street, Arbroath.

The Bruce Oak Heart together again with other reclaimed wood from the original tree from Bruce's Strathleven Estate that was used to frame the bottom part of the Declaration of Arbroath Tapestry. The bottom of the frame depicts the bow of a Birlinn Galley. The side panels open up like sails.

Seals depicting the signatories to the Declaration of Arbroath adorn the Tapestry.

Left: Effigy on display at Arbroath Abbey thought to represent St Thomas Becket.

Following excerpt from: M. Penman, "Sacred Food for the Soul': In Search of the Devotions to Saints of Robert Bruce, King of Scotland, 1306–1329', Speculum, 88 (2013), pp. 1035-1062.

"Similarly, the terminally-ill Robert's halting pilgrimage from Cardross to Whithorn in early 1329, to the shrine of St Ninian, may reflect the presence of that saint's relics at Bannockburn as well as Bruce's Carrick upbringing. Equally, this final journey may have been penitential, echoing Robert's earlier grant to Whithorn Priory 'because of the damage, injury and oppression of the church... by his past wars, and because of the devotion he has to St Ninian.'

Yet, to return to the chronicler's report of Bruce's battle-prayer, it is Robert's bond to the cult of St Thomas Becket, the archbishop of Canterbury martyred in 1170 at the hands of knights of Henry II of England, which stands out. The Bruces had strong family ties to the Canterbury cult and supported the Scottish abbey built for the saint at Arbroath by King William I (the 'Lion') after his capture in battle while invading England.

As the Scottish wars unfolded after 1296 Robert would invest his faith in St Thomas as a symbol of sacrifice, sacrilegious penance and defiance of English royal authority. In 1297 he was obliged to re-swear loyalty to England on one of the swords used to kill Becket, an oath he would soon break. Spurred on by Edward I's death on 7 July 1307 – the Translation feast of Thomas – Robert established his Chancery at Arbroath (under Abbot Bernard) and may have paid for a new tomb effigy for its founder William I.

What few small relics of Thomas were held at Arbroath could thus easily have been at Bannockburn, joined by Becket relics venerated at Glasgow cathedral (shrine of St Kentigern) and those of Columba also held at Arbroath by their hereditary keepers (or 'dewars'). These were thus both strategic and personal acts of worship, arguably as vital a weapon in Bruce's armoury as his war captains and battle-axe."

Bruce Oak Heart with other symbolic replicas,
the Stone of Destiny, Monymusk Reliquary and the Declaration of Arbroath.

The Bruce Oak Heart, views of the Abbey.

Declaration of Arbroath Monument: Dundee Rd, Arbroath.

It is in truth not for glory, nor riches, nor honours that we fight, but for freedom, for that alone, which no honest man gives up but with life itself

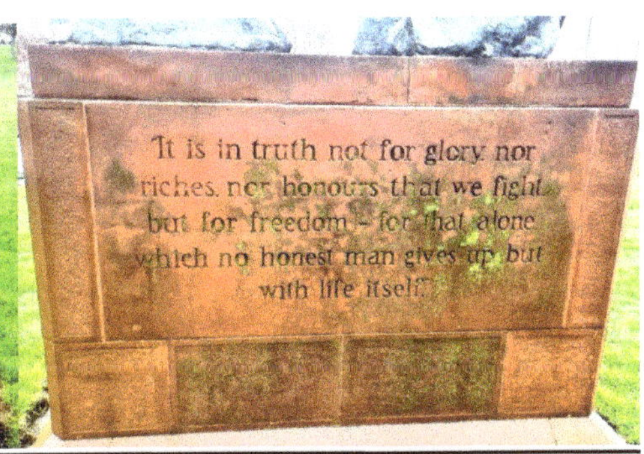

Tour 9, The South West.

Left, Heart Casket ahead of next tour. Right: St John's Tower, Ayr.

St John's Tower, Ayr, In 1315, one year after victory at Bannockburn, in the ancient citadel of Ayr, King Robert held a Parliament here to settle the succession of the throne.
If his only child, Marjorie, did not produce a male heir then his brother, Edward, Earl of Carrick, would succeed Robert to the throne. Bruce held a Parliament at the church on 26th April 1315 to determine the succession of the throne in Scotland.

Bruce's Well, Prestwick.

Bruce's Well, Prestwick.

Robert the Bruce was born in the heart of South Ayrshire at Turnberry Castle on 11th July 1274. He was not in line to be king but after the death of King Alexander III, a long power struggle between the Competitors to the throne led to intervention by King Edward I of England, who subsequently forced the abdication of King John Balliol. When Edward declared himself as Overlord of Scotland, so began the Wars of Independence, the uprisings of Wallace and Moray, culminating in victory for Scotland at Bannockburn.
Bruce's Well, Prestwick, A well has existed on this spot since at least the 13th Century. It served the needs of the community and St Ninian's Church, but particularly the 'Spital and Lazar House', or hospital and leper colony, nearby Bruce benefitted from the Well himself and generously endowed the Lazar House.

Loans.

Soldiers returning from the continent were often afflicted with leprosy. To counter this problem, King Robert set up three leper colonies in the area. A hospital was established at a place now called **St. Quivox.** Loans itself had an Inn (now called Old Loans Inn) and a smiddy (on the site of the petrol station). These places served the lepers of the village.

Crossraguel Abbey.

Founded early in the 13th century by **Duncan, Earl of Carrick**. He invited monks of the Cluniac order from Paisley Abbey to build an Abbey here in his Earldom. The monks of Crossraguel remained loyal to Robert the Bruce throughout the Wars of Independence. As a result, the abbey buildings were severely damaged.

Turnberry Castle, the ancient seat of the Earls of Carrick.

Little remains of this once-impressive fortress - seat of the ancient Earls of Carrick. Robert Bruce was born here on 11th July, 1274. His mother, **Countess Marjorie**, was heiress to the earldom and married Bruce's father in very romantic circumstances it is believed. They produced a large family, all of whom played a major role in the Wars of Independence.

There are two significant historical events connected to Turnberry Castle. On 20 September 1286, several Scottish barons who supported the title of the Bruce as successor of the crown met secretly here. Bruce was only 12 years old at the time.

The second event was the attempt made by Bruce in the spring of 1307, to recover the castle from the English, who were garrisoned there.

This attempt was only partially successful, although ultimately it led to the withdrawal of the English soldiers. His attempt to reclaim the castle marked the beginning of a long road, ending with Bruce's eventual success at Bannockburn.

Bruce ordered the destruction of the castle in 1310, to prevent it from falling once again into the hands of the English.

The castle was nearly destroyed; the ruins that remain are part of the original castle as it does not appear to have been rebuilt.

Home is where the, (Bruce Oak), Heart is.

Kirkoswald, Old Church, South Ayrshire.

Dates back to 1244. It was built by monks who at the same time were founding Crossraguel Abbey, two miles away. The church holds the font in which Bruce was said to have been baptised.

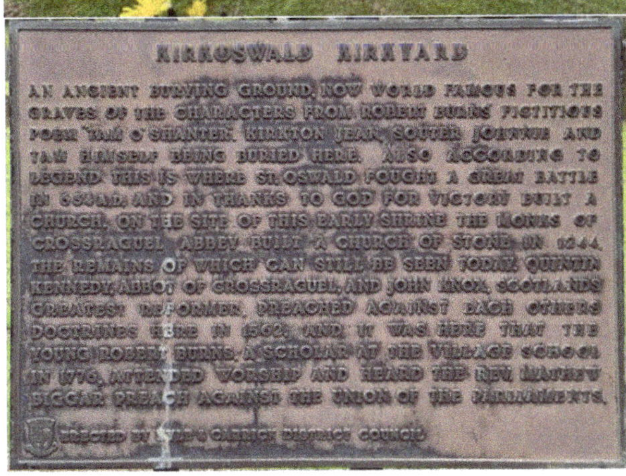

KIRKOSWALD KIRKYARD

AN ANCIENT BURYING GROUND, NOW WORLD FAMOUS FOR THE GRAVES OF THE CHARACTERS FROM ROBERT BURNS FICTITIOUS POEM 'TAM O SHANTER', KIRKTON JEAN, SOUTER JOHNNIE AND TAM HIMSELF BEING BURIED HERE. ALSO ACCORDING TO LEGEND THIS IS WHERE ST. OSWALD FOUGHT A GREAT BATTLE IN 634A.D. AND IN THANKS TO GOD FOR VICTORY BUILT A CHURCH. ON THE SITE OF THIS EARLY SHRINE THE MONKS OF CROSSRAGUEL ABBEY BUILT A CHURCH OF STONE IN 1244, THE REMAINS OF WHICH CAN STILL BE SEEN TODAY. QUINTIN KENNEDY, ABBOT OF CROSSRAGUEL, AND JOHN KNOX, SCOTLAND'S GREATEST REFORMER, PREACHED AGAINST EACH OTHERS DOCTRINES HERE IN 1562. AND IT WAS HERE THAT THE YOUNG ROBERT BURNS, A SCHOLAR AT THE VILLAGE SCHOOL IN 1776, ATTENDED WORSHIP AND HEARD THE REV. MATHEWBIGGAR PREACH AGAINST THE UNION OF THE PARLIAMENTS. ERECTED BY KYLE & CARRICK DISTRICT COUNCIL.

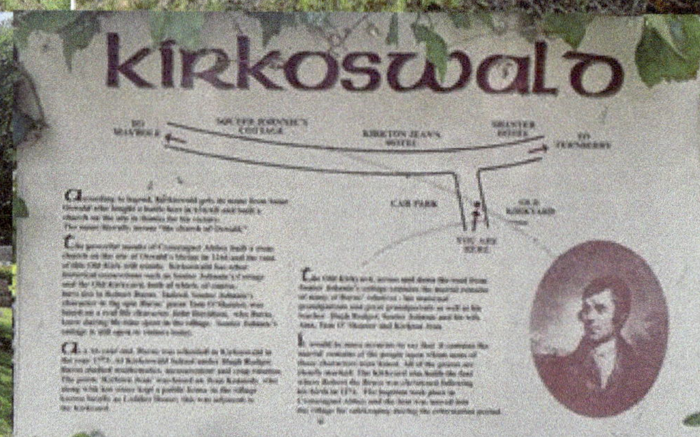
KIRKOSWALD
TO MAYBOLE
SOUTER JOHNNIE'S COTTAGE
KIRKTON JEAN'S HOTEL
SHANTER HOTEL
TO TURNBERRY
CAR PARK
OLD KIRKYARD
YOU ARE HERE

MAIDENS, Ayrshire.

Welcome to Maidens: "Ne'er forget the people", solid advice for the King of Scots.

In February 1307 King Robert returned to take back his kingdom and it was here that he landed. With him, several hundred **Islesmen and Irish supporters**. It nearly ended in disaster when Bruce mistook a fire elsewhere for the beacon to signal his crossing from Arran. But by the end of the night, Bruce had destroyed the English barracks, although his castle at Turnberry remained in English hands. He and his men retreated into the Carrick hills to make camp.

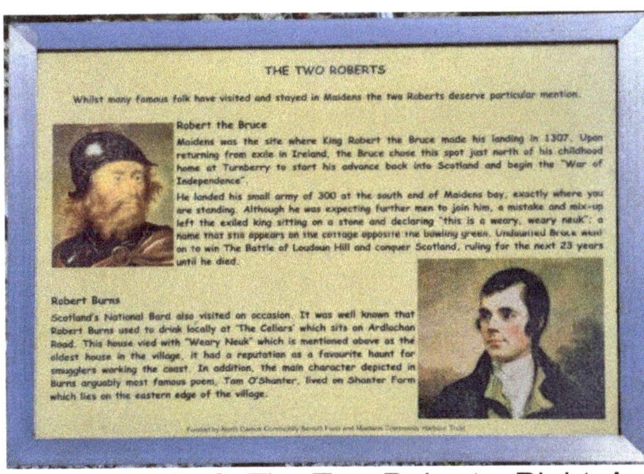

Left: The Two Roberts, Right: Arran Hills from Maidens Harbour.

Plaque Reads:

THE TWO ROBERTS
Whilst many famous folk have visited and stayed in Maidens the two Roberts deserve particular mention.
Robert the Bruce: Maidens was the site where King Robert the Bruce made his landing in 1307. Upon returning from exile in Ireland, the Bruce chose this spot just north of his childhood home at Turnberry to start his advance back into Scotland and begin the "War of Independence".
He landed his small army of 300 at the south end of Maidens bay, exactly where you are standing. Although he was expecting further men to join him, a mistake and mix-up left the exiled king sitting on a stone and declaring "this is a weary, weary neuk"; a name that still appears on the cottage opposite the bowling green. Undaunted Bruce went on to win The Battle of Loudoun Hill and conquer Scotland, ruling for the next 23 years until he died.
Robert Burns: Scotland's National Bard also visited on occasion. It was well known that Robert Burns used to drink locally at The Cellars' which sits on Ardlochan Road. This house vied with "Weary Neuk" which is mentioned above as the oldest house in the village, it had a reputation as a favourite haunt for smugglers working the coast. In addition, the main character depicted in Burns arguably most famous poem, Tam O'Shanter, lived on Shanter Farm which lies on the eastern edge of the village.
Funded by North Carrick Community Benefit Fund and Maidens Community Harbour Trust

Maidens Harbour, Ayrshire, landing site for Bruce after leaving Arran for the mainland.

Chapel Donan.

Hidden in plain sight this ruined chapel is just north of Girvan. It is dedicated to **St Donan of Eigg**, who died c. 617. It was confirmed to the monks of **Crossraguel Abbey** in a charter of Robert III (1390-1406).

Barr & Hadyard Hill.

After the King landed at **Maidens** to restart his campaign for Scotland, his first strike had limited success. He could not retake Turnberry Castle, but made camp in the hills here. He was in a perilous situation and soon became surrounded by English and Scots enemies. From here he crossed into Galloway and confronted the English at **Glentrool** - his first victory.

Loch Ryan.

As it still is today, the loch is a staging point between Scotland and Ulster. Edward I's son, Prince Edward, headed an army along Loch Ryan on September 28, 1301, towards the end of a round trip through Nithsdale and Ayr.

After the dark days of 1306 and the winter spent on Rathlin Island, Bruce divided his forces for a return to the mainland early in 1307. His brothers **Thomas and Alexander** headed one force along with **Malcolm McQuillan, Lord of Kintyre,** and an **Irish sub king** and **Reginald de Crawford.**

The band landed at Loch Ryan from 18 galleys and immediately suffered a disaster. Edward supporter **Dungal Macdouall** and his men of Galloway routed the Bruce party. Only two galleys escaped. Macdouall executed McQuillan and the Irishman on the spot sending their heads to the dying Edward who was at **Lannercost** near Carlisle.

The Bruce brothers and Crawford were taken to Edward who had them drawn at the tails of horses the eight miles to Carlisle where they were hung and beheaded. In January 1317 King Robert sailed from Loch Ryan to Carrickfergus in a bid to shore up his brother Edward's under pressure campaign in Ireland.

The settlements of Cairnryan and Stranraer

Cairnryan was established in the early 18th-century and quickly became an important staging post for coaches on the main road to Ayr from the south.

Located around 6 miles north of Stranraer on the A77, nowadays, many travellers pass through Cairnryan en route to or from Northern Ireland on the ferry.

Views around Loch Ryan

When Bruce returned to the mainland to start his campaign at Maidens, its landscape provided shelter and hiding places, and access to the sea was crucial in supplying men, ships and support for his cause.

In February 1307 he sent his brothers, Thomas and Alexander, south to head inland and cut off the English supply chain coming in from Dumfries.

However, when they landed near Stranraer on the shores of Loch Ryan to attack the English supply route from Carlisle, they were betrayed and attacked by the Macdowalls, Bruce's enemies in Galloway.

Thomas and Alexander were handed over to the English and executed in Carlisle without trial.

Clatteringshaws.

In March 1307 King Robert hid out in the hills around Moss Raploch and Glentrool. An English army camped here was set upon by the Scots at dawn and, as the Scots picked over the dead for weapons and booty, the king rested against a large stone, known as the Bruce Stone. The battle site itself is now submerged by the reservoir but the stone can be visited in Galloway Forest Park.

Plaque reads:

CLATTERINGSHAWS DAM, CONSTRUCTED BY THE GALLOWAY WATER POWER COMPANY: 1932-34.
CLATTERINGSHAWSDAM AND THE LOCH OCCUPY GROUND MEMORABLE IN SCOTTISH HISTORY: CLOSE BY THE DAM THE OLD EDINBURGH ROAD LEADING TO **WHITHORN (CANDIDA CASA IV-Vth CENTURY)** THE EARLIEST CHRISTIAN FOUNDATION IN SCOTLAND.
THE WATERS OF THE LOCH ARE GATHERED FROM THE FASTNESSES OF THE DUNGEON OF BUCHAN AND FROM THE SITE OF THAT ANCIENT FOREST OF BUCHAN WHERE ROBERT BRUCE WAS HARD PRESSED BY HIS ENEMIES AFTER HIS RETURN TO SCOTLAND FROM RATHLIN IN 1307.
A VICTORY GAINED NEAR THIS PLACE BY ROBERT BRUCE, OR HIS BROTHER EDWARD, IS COMMEMORATED BY THE GREAT BOULDER KNOWN AS THE KING'S OR BRUCE'S STONE WHICH STANDS NEAR THE SHORES OF THE LOCH 700 YARDS NORTH OF CLATTERINGSHAWS FARM.
MARY QUEEN OF SCOTS PASSED THIS WAY ON 13TH AUGUST 1566. THE SURROUNDING WILDS WERE SOUGHT AS A REFUGE BY THE COVENANTERS DURING THEIR STRUGGLES IN THE SEVENTEETH CENTURY.

The Bruce Stone, Clatteringshaws.

Glentrool.

Is the scene of King Robert's first significant victory over the English: in April 1307, he hid in these hills with no more than around 300 men, waiting for the chance to pounce on his prey. At Glentrool he lured the Earl of Pembroke and 1,500 heavy English cavalry along the narrow track on the south side of Loch Trool, bombarded them with rocks and debris, then fell on them as they scattered.

The Scots buried the defeated English Soldiers at the eastern end of Loch Trool, near to the slope where Bruce's force attacked them, at a place now known as 'Soldiers Holm', see centre of photo. 'Holm' being an area of flat ground by a river which is submerged in times of flood.

From Historical Environment Scotland:

Bruce's Stone, Loch Trool

A commemorative monument, dated 1929, consisting of a large, single piece of Loch Doon granite set on a base of smaller granite stones which are cemented together. It is situated on an elevated and prominent position on the north side of Loch Trool, overlooking the loch. A polished area on the north face of the large boulder is inscribed:

'In loyal remembrance of Robert the Bruce, King of Scots, whose victory in this glen over an English force in March 1307, opened the campaign of independence which he brought to a decisive close at Bannockburn on 24 June 1314.'
The south face is inscribed ***'Unveiled 5 June 1929'.***

Statement of Special Interest

Bruce's Stone is a large and distinctive granite monument erected in 1929 to commemorate one of the first victories of Robert the Bruce over the English at the beginning of the Wars of Independence. It is constructed from locally available granite and was designed to reference the battle, which was traditionally thought to be won by Bruce's men throwing boulders on to the English troops.

The monument has a spectacular unaltered setting on the north side of Loch Trool and overlooks the probable site of the battle. It can also be read as evidence for the wider 20th century Scottish nationalist movement, which was gathering momentum during the 1920s.

Age and Rarity.

This granite monument was erected on 5 June 1929 to commemorate the victory of Robert the Bruce at the Battle of Glen Trool in 1307 and was paid for by public subscription. 1929 was the 600th anniversary of Bruce's death and the erection of this memorial was one of a number of events in the country at the time to mark the occasion.
A report in the **Galloway Gazette of 15 June 1929** notes that a crowd of over 300 spectators attended the ceremony, including the historian Sir Herbert Maxwell and Professor Robert Rait, the Historiographer Royal for Scotland and Professor of Scottish History and Literature at Glasgow University from 1913-1929.

The newspaper also reports that a leaden casket containing ancient and modern coins was placed beneath the large boulder. A report in the **Dundee Evening Telegraph of 15 May 1929** records a number of events that were organised around the country for the 600th anniversary of Bruce's death, including commemorations at **Cardross Castle** in Dumbarton where Bruce died, and at the **Borestone, at the field of Bannockburn**, near Stirling.

A bronze statue of Bruce in a niche at the gatehouse of Edinburgh Castle was also unveiled as part of these commemorations. The Battle of Glen Trool, considered more of a skirmish by some historians, took place around **March/April 1307** and was an early victory for Robert the Bruce in his fight for Scottish independence from the English and Edward I in the campaign known as the First Wars of Independence.

The inscription on the stone states that the battle at Glen Trool opened the campaign and that it terminated with the Battle of Bannockburn in 1314. The wars did not finally end, however, until the signing of the **Edinburgh-Northampton Treaty** in **1328,** which recognised Scotland as an independent kingdom.

In 1306, Robert the Bruce crowned himself King of Scotland and a number of battles and skirmishes followed between Bruce and his supporters and those who opposed his claim, including Edward I of England. Following defeats in 1306 at **Methven** (Perthshire) and **Dail Righ** (*Ayrshire).

(JG correction: Dail Righ, *Perthshire - not Dalry in Ayrshire).

Bruce went into hiding, possibly to the Western Isles. He returned to the mainland in 1307 to fight for his claim and he eventually established a camp at Glen Trool. Bruce used guerrilla type warfare tactics at this point, hiding himself in the hills and making it hard for the English troops to know his exact whereabouts.

They were aware of his presence in the area, however, as a previous skirmish at **Moss Raploch**, now on the east side of **Clatteringshaws Loch**, had ended with victory for Bruce. A large erratic boulder at the site (currently owned by the National Trust of Scotland) is also named **Bruce's Stone** and is traditionally thought to be where he rested after the battle.

At **Glen Trool**, Bruce gained advantage over the English troops, who were led by the **Earl of Pembroke,** by taking higher ground.

Popular tradition tells that Bruce ambushed the English soldiers by throwing boulders down on them. Taken by surprise, the English troops fled. Bruce's Stone is positioned to overlook the most likely site of the battle.
The anniversary of Robert the Bruce's death saw a number of monuments erected to commemorate his significance in Scottish history.
An equestrian statue in Stirling, one of the most significant monuments to Bruce, came slightly later for the 650th anniversary of the Battle of Bannockburn. It is listed at category A (LB49860). Bruce's Stone can also be placed in the wider context of the period.

The 1920s was a significant period in memorialisation and commemoration following the huge impact of the First World War. The Scottish National War memorial was opened in 1927, and by this date thousands of memorials to Scotland's fallen, varying in scale and architectural ambition, had been erected in every community across the country.

While the design of the Bruce's Stone monument is informal, its concept - built up of large stones found in the area – directly reflects how the battle is thought to have been fought with **boulders** (see below). Its setting and location also add significantly to its special interest (see below).

Moreover, Bruce's Stone can also be considered an important marker of the contemporary growing interest in Scottish nationalism and national identity, as it was erected shortly after the **Scottish National Party** was founded in **1928.**

Architectural or Historic Interest
Technological excellence or innovation, material or design quality
The monument is made of erratic **Loch Doon granite**.
This granite originates from the Loch Doon area of Ayrshire and information from The British Geological Survey on SCRAN notes that erratic boulders of Loch Doon granite can be found in a wide surrounding area as they were moved by glacial activity.
It is likely, therefore, that the boulders used for this monument were found locally.
There were a number of granite quarries in Dumfries and Galloway, particularly in the 19th and early 20th centuries.

The local firm, **Galloway Granite**, was established in 1928 by a Mackenzie family who were stone masons.
The report of the unveiling of the stone in the **Galloway Gazette of 15 June, 1929** notes that the sculptor for the stone was a Mr Mackenzie.
The design of the monument, using small boulders as a base and a large boulder on top, is a direct reference to the tradition that Bruce won the battle by sending boulders down onto the English troops.

The monument sits on a natural rocky pavement and the use of local stone can be interpreted as conscious design decision to link the monument, and therefore Bruce, to the Galloway Hills.
Whilst the choice of materials is an important feature of the monument, the overall design is not exceptional in architectural terms.
Other monuments to Bruce, for example the equestrian statue at Bannockburn (listed at category A) have more detailed architectural elements.

Setting
The monument is situated on an elevated and remote spot on the north side of Loch Trool, with far-reaching views to the east and west along the loch. It is situated in an unaltered, prominent and spectacular setting across the Loch from the most likely site of the battle and its position is therefore an important part of its interest.

Close Historical Associations
The criteria for listing state that close historical associations with nationally important people, or events whose associations are well-documented, where the physical fabric is also of some quality and interest, can be a significant factor.

The fabric should also reflect the person or event. The Bruce's Stone monument was erected to commemorate King Robert the Bruce, King of Scotland from 1306-1329, who secured Scotland's independence from England and was a nationally important figure in the history of Scotland.

The fabric and design of the monument is relevant to the battle.

Bruce's Stone, Loch Trool (LB52395) (historicenvironment.scot)

Creebridge.

The flat estuary here is the site of an indecisive battle between Edward I and Scottish forces led by Edward, Earl of Buchan. On seeing the English army bearing down on them, the Scots cavalry fled for the hills, but the English were ill-prepared to make pursuit over this terrain, so most Scots escaped. The River Cree was the limit of Edward's 1300 invasion and, starved of funds, he returned home.

The River Cree at Newton Stewart, the base for exploring Dumfries & Galloway.

Dalswinton Castle.

On 10 February 1306 **John Comyn** set out from Dalswinton Castle to meet Robert Bruce at **Greyfriars Monastery, Dumfries**. A few hours later, Comyn lay dead and Bruce seized Dumfries Castle. The present Dalswinton House stands on the site of Comyn's medieval castle. It is a private home, not open to the public.

Dalswinton Castle was perhaps once a very substantial border fortress which occupied a large natural mound overlooking the River Nith.
The strategic value of the site known since Roman times, it seems likely that it was the site of a fort of the lords of Nithsdale in the 12th century.
The estate passed to the **Comyn** family by marriage, perhaps in the reign of Alexander II, and it is probably due to the Comyns that the substantial castle was built here, the walls of which may have been up to 4.5 metres thick.

It was repeatedly targeted in the early 14th century Wars of Independence, and probably never brought back into use after Robert Bruce dismantled it in 1313.
It may have been repaired, or replaced, by the Stewart family of Garlies in the early 15th century, and by the 16th century a tower and courtyard were occupied by the Stewarts here.

In the early 17th century the Stewarts sold Dalswinton, and a new tower house was built on low ground, itself to be removed and a single tower left as a garden feature when the Miller family erected the new mansion on top of the mound.
Today this house and estate are private and the gardens open one day a year through the Scotland's Gardens scheme.

Dumfries.

HERE STOOD THE MONASTERY
OF THE GREY FRIARS WHERE ON THURSDAY 10TH FEBRUARY
1306 ROBERT THE BRUCE
AIDED BY SIR ROGER KIRKPATRICK
SLEW THE RED COMYN AND OPENED THE FINAL STAGE
OF THE WAR FOR SCOTTISH INDEPENDENCE
WHICH ENDED VICTORIOUSLY ON THE FIELD OF BANNOCKBURN
1314
'I MAK SICCAR '
ERECTED BY THE CITIZENS OF
DUMFRIES & THE SALTIRE SOCIETY.

'Comyn's End', 95 Friars Vennel, Dumfries. Friars' Vennel plaque Reads: *'The alignment of these buildings is approximately that of the early Greyfriars Monastery Wall. As you reach the ridge on which the ancient burgh stood you will see the statue of Robert Burns overlooked by the elegant 180ft spire of Greyfriars (the "new") church'.*

Below: **Comyn's Court** sign,

Greyfriars' Street, Dumfries.

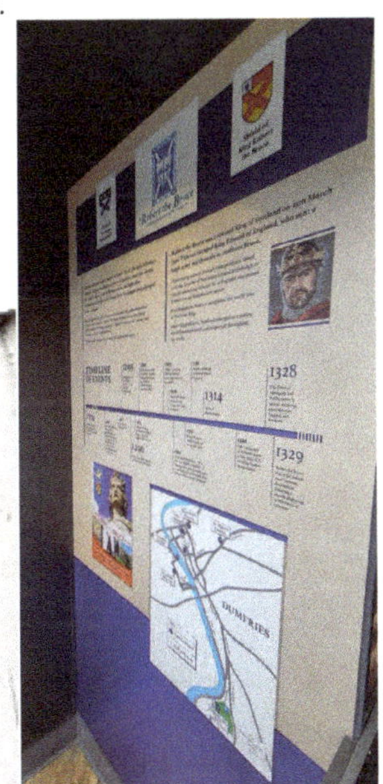

Right: The local Greggs in Dumfries has an info board in its window.

'The Robert The Bruce' displays a poem about Bruce.

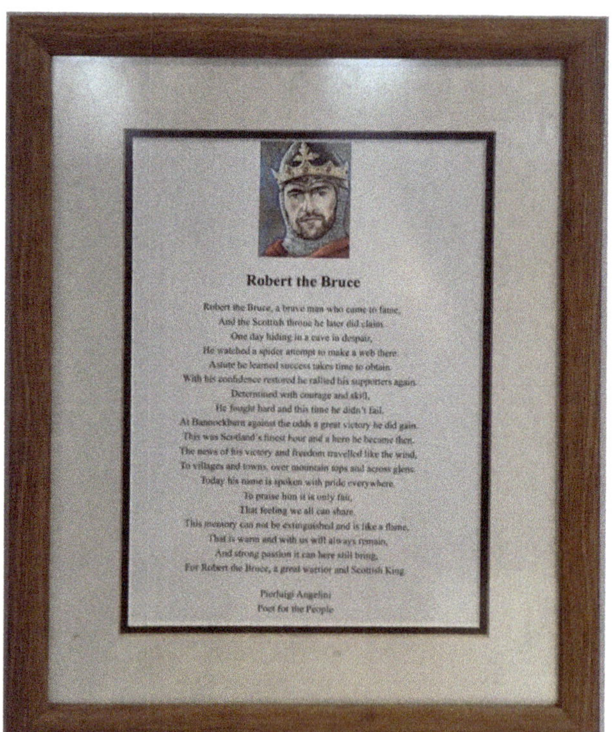

Robert the Bruce

Robert the Bruce, a brave man who came to fame
And the Scottish throne he later did claim
One day hiding in a cave in despair,
He watched a spider attempt to make a web there.
Astute he learned success takes time to obtain
With his confidence restored he rallied his supporters again
Determined with courage and skill,
He fought hard and this time he didn't fail
At Bannockburn against the odds a great victory he did gain.
This was Scotlandss finest hour and a hero he became then.
The news of of his victory and freedom travelled like the wind
To villages and towns, over mountain tops and across glens.
Today his name is spoken with pride everywhere
To praise him it is only fair
That feeling we all can share.
This memory can not be extinguished and is like a flame.
That is warm and with us will always remain
And strong passion it can here still bring.
For Robert the Bruce, a great warrior and Scottish King

Pierluigi Angelini
Poet for the People

Dumfries Castle.

Steps leading up to Castle Hill site of Dumfries Castle.

Bruce Oak Heart at Dumfries Castle Marker Stone, Castledykes Park.

Left: Flag and Castle Marker Stone.
Right: Plaque commemorating Bruce's attack on the castle after killing John Comyn.

KING ROBERT THE BRUCE
ON 10TH February 1306
CAPTURED THE CASTLE OF DUMFRIES
WHICH OCCUPIED THIS SITE AND SO BEGAN THE WAR WHICH VINDICATED
SCOTLAND'S INDEPENDENCE
THIS MEMORIAL STONE
LAID 10TH FEBRUARY 1906 BY WILLIAM MURRAY ESQUIRE… OF DUMFRIESHIRE.

Left: Panel depicting Bruce's attack on Dumfries Castle. Right: Bruce Wood Sculpture, Castledykes Park.

Dumfries Museum.

Left: Meeting with Tom Hughes at Dumfries Museum, here he holds the symbolic Bruce Oak Heart. Tom, as part of The Medieval Bruce Heritage Trust, helped organise Dumfries & Galloway's own celebration of Bruce's anniversary with a series of events with local communities across the region.
Right: Tom explained the history of the **Pilgrims Badge** on display - on the right hand side, it's a rare example of a 14th Century pilgrim's badge from St Ninian's Shrine, Whithorn.

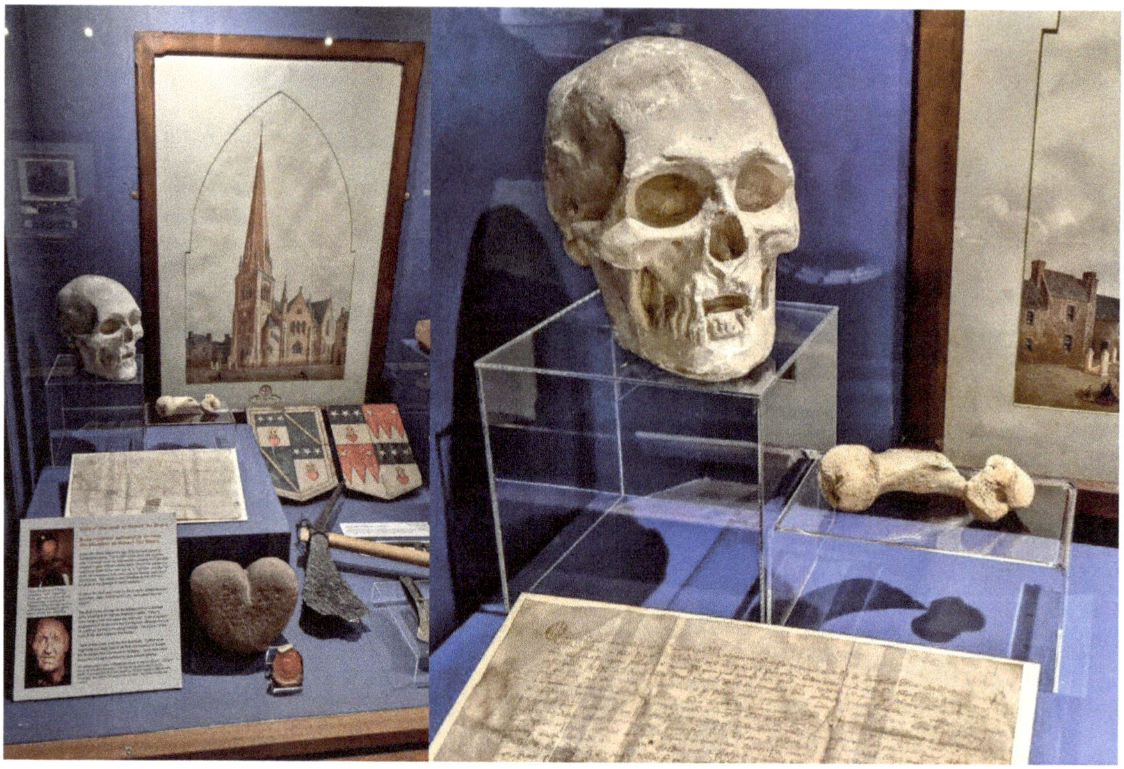

Cast of Bruce's skull, the two bones to the right of it are purported to be from the top part of his thigh bone and his foot.

From Museum Website:
"...Robert the Bruce, top of his femur and section of his foot.
This bone material is part of a bone from the foot and part of the lower end of a thigh bone.
The cast of a skull, along with these fragments of bone material said to have been taken from the skeleton of Robert the Bruce in 1818, were presented to Dumfries Museum in 1996.
They had belonged to Wallace Black, a Dumfries man. Family tradition has it that he was given the cast and the bone material by a friend who was present when the skeleton was discovered.
Bone fragments and teeth from the skeleton of Robert the Bruce are held by other organisations and individuals in Scotland.
In the past such relics were treated with great respect and were believed to have special powers.
Perhaps today is seems more appropriate that they should be reburied?
After his death in 1329 Bruce's body was interred in Dunfermline Abbey.
The site of the tomb was lost, possibly when the abbey was damaged by Protestant religious demonstrations in the 1500s.
In 1818 workmen making repairs to the Abbey discovered a skeleton that had been wrapped in gold cloth within a stone tomb.
This was examined by Robert Liston, an Edinburgh surgeon.
Bruce had wanted his heart to be taken to the Holy Lands, or Palestine, in order to fulfil his ambition to take part in the Crusades.
After his death his breastbone had been sawn away so that the heart could be removed.
Liston identified the skeleton as that of Bruce because of damage to the breastbone.
A cast of the skull was made by the sculptor, William Scoular, and is now kept in the Anatomy Department of the University of Edinburgh.
Further casts were taken from this original cast.
No portraits were made of Robert the Bruce during his lifetime.
Perhaps the most accurate likeness of him can be reconstructed from his skull?
Recently this was attempted by a team of forensic scientists.
The skull shows damage to the left eye socket and cheek bone, possibly from injuries received in battle.
There is bone missing from the upper jaw and nose. It has long been suggested that Bruce suffered from leprosy, although there is no evidence for this in historical records.
However, the erosion of the bone of the skull supports this conclusion.
It could be that Bruce's status as king meant that his illness was not made public.
People with leprosy had to live apart from others and this would not have been possible for a king.

St Mary's Church, 1, St Mary's Street, Dumfries.

The church stands on the execution site of **Sir Christopher Seaton**, (1278–1306).
English born, he held lands in England and Scotland and was a supporter of Robert the Bruce.
In 1301, at the age of twenty-three, he married Bruce's sister **Christian**, (or Christina).
Seton was present on 10th February 1306 when **Sir John, The Red Comyn of Badenoch** was stabbed by Bruce in **Greyfriars Church**, Dumfries.
As Sir Robert Comyn rushed to aid his nephew, Seton struck him down with a blow to the head.
A letter of excommunication was issued naming the Earl of Carrick and three other knights, Sir Alexander Lindsay, Sir Christopher and his brother John Seton as John Comyn's killers.

Seton was also present at the coronation of Bruce and some accounts have him present at the Battle of Methven on 19 June 1306 - but Duncan places him at Loch Doon Castle, an important castle for the Earls of Carrick and one of three that Robert tried to retain
Loch Doon fell about the 14th of August when it was besieged by the English.
After the surrender of the castle by its Governor Sir Gilbert de Carrick, Seton was hanged, drawn and quartered at Dumfries in accordance with Edward I's policy of giving no quarter to Scottish prisoners.
Seton's Cumberland estates, with the exception of his mother's dower, were given to Sir Robert de Clifford.
A small chapel was raised at the site of his execution by his wife Christian to the memory of her husband in 1326.

The small plaque on a 19thC memorial reads:

'These stones, relics of the ancient chapel dedicated to The Holy Rood endowed by King Robert The Bruce. In memory of Sir Christopher or Chrystal Seatoun are here placed by Major James Adair 1840.'

Lochmaben.

In medieval times, forest and marsh forced travellers from England up through **Annandale** towards Lochmaben, and it was a key point of conflict between England and Scotland. The Bruces built a motte and bailey castle which survives today as part of the golf course. The later Castle built at Castle Loch was begun by Edward I of England c. 1300.

The hill on which stood the original '*Old* Lochmaben Castle' of the Bruces.

The ruins of the *New* Lochmaben Castle lie south of the town of Lochmaben within the feudal Lordship of Annandale, and the united county of Dumfries and Galloway.

It was built by Edward I in the 14th century, (replacing the earlier motte and bailey castle of the Bruces, Lords of Annandale).

Edward I replaced the older motte and bailey castle with a much stronger structure at the southern end of **Castle Loch** around 1300 and its remains still show the massive strength of its defences.

Archibald Douglas, Lord of Galloway, with the assistance of the Earls of March and Douglas, after a siege of nine days, took Lochmaben Castle from the English and "razed it to the ground" on 4 February 1384/5.

Ruins of 'New' Lochmaben Castle and nearby Bruce Tree Carving.

When the Bruce family motte was destroyed by the river at Annan, the family moved to Lochmaben. The date of the construction is not known, but the Motte was recorded to be in existence in 1166 and in 1173 when William the Lion held the 'castle' of Lochmaben.

It became the *Caput,* (Latin for Head), of Annandale by 1204 and the last mention of it is in 1315-21 when King Robert I granted the lands of Mouswald to Thomas de Carruthers - the *reddendo,* (a clause in a charter specifying the particular duty or service due from a vassal to his superior), was a pair of gilt spurs to be delivered *"apud manerium nostrum de Lochmaben"* (at our manor of Lochmaben).

It is thought that King Edward stayed here on 4th-5th September 1298. The 'old' original castle of Lochmaben stood between the Castle Loch and the Kirk Loch, upon a natural eminence, of from twelve to fourteen acres, close to the town, a well-chosen spot, overlooking a great expanse of country, and from which, notwithstanding the thick forests which then surrounded it, the motions of an enemy could be easily watched.

The town likely owes its origin to the choice of this site for a stronghold. This ancient fortress was surrounded by deep dry moats, still distinctly traceable.

The fortress was initially supplied by water from a spring nearby but a greater supply was piped in from the rising grounds near where St Thomas's Chapel stood about a mile and a half to the west, on the A709 Dumfries Road, in leaden pipes.

In the early to mid-1800s three pieces were revealed, one within the present enclosure at the south-west corner, the other in the adjoining park, and the third while a ditch was being cut through a moss, about midway between the castle and the spring.

That spring still discharges a supply of pure water on the farm of St Thomas; (now Hunter House Farm) and close beside it there is another fountain called the Baptism Well.

It is also said that there was an orchard planted on the slope from the castle down to the Kirk Loch.

The 'Bruce motte at Lochmaben now stands on the golf course and has been greatly altered by subsequent landscaping.

As a result of tee-building operations on Lochmaben Golf Course in November 1966, 27 fragments of pottery with fragments of heavy unglazed tile, oyster shells, and animal bone were recovered. These were dated to the late 12th-early 13th century.

Finds of medieval pottery and tiles suggest that it continued in occupation into the 14th century 26. Probably it remained in use until the stone castle on the loch replaced it.

Ericstane.

In February 1306, at a place a mile or so north of the town known as the *'Arrickstone'*, Bruce had a historic meeting. Riding north for Glasgow, having killed John The Red Comyn at Greyfriars Monastery, Dumfries, his party halted here at the **Devil's Beeftub**. Waiting for him and his entourage as they made their way to the coronation at Scone was an olive skinned, dark haired young man called **James Douglas** carrying a message of support from **Bishop Lamberton of St. Andrews.**

Douglas, out to recover his lands and avenge the death of his father, Sir William, paid homage to Bruce and went on from there to become one of his most trusted lieutenants and foremost knights in Europe at that time. Douglas pledged his loyalty to the would-be king - a promise he kept all his life. He was known as "the guid Sir James" in Scotland the 'the Black Douglas' south of the Border.

Ericstane and the Devil's Beeftub, a landscape fit for heroes.

Here Robert the Bruce & James Douglas first met.

Castle Douglas.

Castle Douglas is the scene of a massacre in 1308 when Sir James Douglas raided the south west. The town was under the English command of Robert Clifford. Douglas killed most defenders and destroyed the fortifications. The nearby castle at Threave was attacked by Edward Bruce in the same year. The present Threave Castle was built by Douglas' son, Archibald the Grim.

St Bride's Chapel, Douglas.

St Bride's Chapel, site of the tomb for Sir James Douglas, renowned as one of Scotland's Greatest Warriors. The partial remains of St Bride's Church stand in the village of Douglas close to the Douglas Water. Also sometimes known as *Old St Bride's Church,* (to avoid confusion with the current parish church, also dedicated to St Bride).

ST BRIDE'S CHURCH, DOUGLAS.
'Mausoleum of the Black Douglases'

This ruin was once the parish church of Douglas. The remains consist of the choir, (housing the altar), and the south aisle of the nave - both late 14th century in date - with a clock tower added in the 16th century.

The clock, dating from 1565, is probably the oldest working in Scotland. The choir was re-roofed in the 19th century. Douglasdale was the original power - base of the 'Black' Douglases. Modest landowners in the 15th century, they gained enormously through their support of Robert the Bruce during the Wars of Independence with England in the early 14th century. By 1400, they were the most powerful family in southern Scotland.

But this position brought them into conflict with the Stewart king, James II, and in 1455 they were overthrown. Their castle at Douglas was finally destroyed by fire in 1755, but a tangible reminder of them still exists here, for the parish church became their mausoleum. Three fine wall tombs survive in the choir, together with memorials from more recent times.
HISTORIC SCOTLAND

The Bruce Oak Heart at St Bride's Chapel, the clock, dating from 1565, is probably the oldest working in Scotland.

The Bruce Oak Heart: a symbolic journey from
The Church of the Holy Sepulchre in Jerusalem to the Tomb of Sir James Douglas.

'Wend on as thou was wont
Throw the batell in bront,
Ay formast in the front
Thy fays amang!
And I sall followe the in faith, or feye to be fellit.
As thi legeman leile, my lyking thow art.'

R. Holland, The Buke of the Howlat, ll. 491-6

St Bride's Chapel Alter.

Tour 10, Bruce's final Pilgrimage.

GIRVAN.

In the years after Bannockburn, the King spent much time in Ayrshire and the Southwest of Scotland. In his final year, he made a pilgrimage through these lands down to Whithorn in Galloway. Around this time, he held Court in Girvan and granted a Charter to the Friars of Ayr.

A plaque on the wall of **Knockcushan House** commemorates the event.

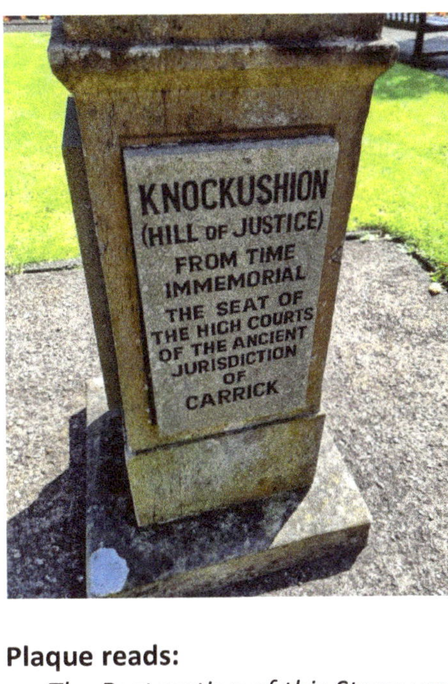

Plaque reads:

The Restoration of this Stone was the gift of the SOROPTIMIST CLUB of GIRVAN and DISTRICT In the Club's 10th Anniversary Year to mark the occasion of the TERCENTENARY of GIRVAN.

Glenluce Abbey, founded around 1192.

Bruce stayed at Glenluce Abbey in Galloway on his painful pilgrimage to St Ninian's shrine in Whithorn between February and April 1329, shortly before his death.

The Cistercian monks here probably came from Dundrennan Abbey, near Kirkcudbright. They brought with them an austere way of life - but also the splendour of their architecture. Glenluce Abbey came into State care in 1933, and during clearance of the rubble, many artefacts were discovered, now on display in the visitor centre. When King Robert made his final journey to Whithorn, he travelled down the coast, resting at several places along the way including Glenluce Abbey.

Glenluce Abbey was founded in about 1192 by **Roland, Lord of Galloway**. He asked Cistercian monks from Dundrennan Abbey near Kirkcudbright to set up a daughter-house here.

The first designated Abbot of Glenluce, whose name is unknown, would have arrived with twelve of the white-robed Cistercian monks and simply set to work clearing the site and building the abbey. The first stage was to build the east end of the church, so that worship could take place. The remainder of the abbey church and the domestic buildings of the abbey then followed.

In common with other abbeys, work would have continued for many decades and once built, the abbey would have been subject to a fairly continuous series of renovations, extensions and revisions during an active life that continued over a period of some four hundred years.

The most important part of the abbey was the **Abbey Church**. This was usually constructed along the north side of the site so that its taller height did not cast the rest of the abbey in shadow. Today parts of the south transept wall still stand, but little remains above ground level of the rest of the church.

To the south of the abbey church most of the other buildings in the complex were grouped around three sides of a square cloister, where the monks would walk and pass their time in silent contemplation. Today by far the best preserved parts of Glenluce Abbey lay on the east side of the cloister, part of which has been restored to give an idea of how the whole area would have looked and felt.

Behind the restored portion of cloister is the chapter house. This was the second most important space within the abbey, where meetings took place and business was conducted.

The structure on view today was probably rebuilt in about 1515. The windows were restored in the 1900s.

Above the chapter house would have been the spartan accommodation for perhaps 15 monks, while on the other side of the cloister was a range in which lay-brethren lived.

The fourth side of the cloister, the south range, originally comprised the refectory and kitchen, but was later converted into a house. The foundations of a variety of outbuildings can be seen further to the south, while the more modern buildings to the north-west also house a small museum.

Glenluce's position saved it from the repeated destruction that befell so many abbeys further east, but it still suffered from its fair share of disputes over land rights and ownership.

One of these in 1544 led to the eviction of the monks, who then spent a year in temporary accommodation in Maybole in Ayrshire before the argument was settled.

The end of Glenluce's active life as a monastery came with the Reformation in 1560. The monks who accepted the new doctrines were allowed to live out their days in the abbey, the last one dying in 1602. Part of the site was then converted into a house before being re-acquired by the church in 1619 for use as a manse.

Over the following 300 years the abbey remains deteriorated through the forces of nature and through their use as a quarry for nearby building projects. Glenluce Abbey passed into State care in 1933 and is today looked after by Historic Environment Scotland.

Chapel Finian

The remaining ruins of the chapel consists of a small 10th- or 11th-century building within a stone-walled enclosure, close to the shore on the raised beach at Corwall Port.

Built in the AD 900s or 1000s, probably as a resting spot for pilgrims on their way to Whithorn Priory it was built in the Irish style, and is very simple, comprising a single rectangular room.

The chapel is named after the Irish saint Finnian, the scholar and monastic founder who is said to have taught St Columba. Some scholars believe that Finnian is a corruption of Uinniau.

Uinniau was a bishop in the 500s and established churches in Ireland and south-west Scotland. Uinniau is also thought to be the real historical figure behind St Ninian, whose cult is closely associated with nearby Whithorn.

Judging from parallels in Ireland, Chapel Finian was probably built in the 900s or 1000s – though it's possible it was not the first chapel on this site.
It was probably a resting place for pilgrims, mostly travelling from Ireland on their way to Whithorn Priory. It's easy to imagine the gratitude felt by earlier travellers and pilgrims arriving here by boat.

Excavations in 1950 revealed that the chapel consisted of a single rectangular room, about 6.7m by 4.1m, with an entrance through a door in the south wall. Little evidence of the internal arrangements were found, other than traces of wall plaster and a stone bench encased in wood. A drystone wall surrounds the church. Healing properties were probably ascribed to the chapel's well, which survives within the chapel grounds.

Chapen Finian is named for the Irish saint Finnian, a great scholar and founder who is said to have taught St Columba. He was educated at Whithorn and died about AD 579. Some scholars believe that Finian and Ninian are corruptions of the name Uinniau. Uinniau was a bishop active in the 500s and was probably the real historical figure on whom the cults of Finian and Ninian are based.

The chapel stands as a monument within the spiritual landscape of pilgrimage to the shrine of St Ninian at Whithorn.

Info Board reads:

"...This small chapel, named after Findbar, (see my notes on the Chapel name in the comments of the previous pic), a 6th century Irish saint. Its bleak position on this exposed cost is due to the nearby beach's use as a landing place for pilgrims.

They were going to the shrine of St. Ninian at Whithorn, particularly those from Ireland.
Chapels of this type were common in Ireland at the time.

The chapel is very simple, comprising a single rectangular room, entered from a door in the south wall. The walls are built of large, roughly-dressed stones bonded with mortar.

The two long walls are buttressed. Excavations in 1950 found little evidence of the internal arrangements, although there were traces of a stone bench, perhaps encased in wood, along the eastern part of the side wall.

A dry stone perimeter wall surrounded the site, which was characteristic of early Christian churches. It enclosed a house for the priest, probably timber built, a well (which still survives) and a burial ground.

The chapel must have been a welcome refuge after a tough sea crossing."

Left: Chapel Finian, looking southwest-wards where Ireland lies. This was a landing point for Irish Pilgrims on their way to Whithorn.

Right: Chapel Finian Well.

The Laggangairn Standing Stones: In the footsteps of medieval pilgrims.

Located on the Southern Upland Way in a remote moorland area. These two standing stones are believed to be the only survivors of a circle of 14 stones, with seven still standing in 1873. The stones are only two feet apart and are carved with Christian crosses dating between AD 600 and 8001. Pilgrims stopped here on their way to Whithorn Chapel marking the prehistoric stones with crosses.

Further info on the Laggangairn Stones (mentioned in the previous pic of info board at St Ninian's Chapel, Isle of Whithorn).

They are located on the modern day Southern Upland Way in a remote moorland area in Galloway. Pilgrims stopped here on their way to Whithorn marking the prehistoric stones with crosses as a 'way finder'.
The Stones were likely erected about 2000 BC. These two standing stones are believed to be the only survivors of a circle of 14 stones. Seven were recorded to be still standing in 1873 after around 4000 years.

The others were removed over the centuries, some for use as lintels in neighbouring cottages. These remaining stones are only two feet apart and are each carved with a large Christian cross surrounded by four 'crosslets'.

The style of the crosses suggests they were added during the AD 600s and 800s. The name of the nearby farm of Kilgallioch, translated as 'church of the standing stones', suggests there may have been an early church site just to the north.

A writer in 1907 also mentions three beehive holy wells near this spot. This remote spot seems to have been a sacred place for thousands of years.

Monreith.

Monreith is a tiny coastal settlement on the west of the Machars in Wigtownshire.

Bruce stayed there on his final pilgrimage to St Ninian's shrine at Whithorn in March, 1329.

It is a small seaside village in the Machars, 2.5 miles south of Port William. The village is near a long sandy beach which is popular with visitors and holiday makers.

It has rock pools and interesting caves, synonymous with the area, one of which is streaked red and known as the 'Butcher's Cave'.

St Ninian's Cave.

The Bruce Oak Heart, carved from the tree that once stood in the King's Strathleven Estate, reaches St Ninians Cave the location of the early origins of Christianity in Scotland.
It's not hard to imagine Bruce making the effort to visit the cave and, on his arrival, looking out towards this view of the stony shoreline.

A cross marked stone found on the shoreline.

Whithorn Priory, Dumfries & Galloway.

In 1328 Bruce had secured independence from England, but he was a dying man. At the age of 54, his body was wracked with An illness after a lifetime of harsh living. In April 1329, he made a last pilgrimage from his home at Cardross to Whithorn to pray at St Ninian's Shrine. He was pious and prayed for forgiveness for the murder of John Comyn, and for the suffering and death of his loved ones.
The award-winning Whithorn Story tells the story of Whithorn's early Christian past, the churches on the site and the archaeology discovered there during the last century.

Above: Signs for King's Road, & for Priory & Museum from Whithorn High Street.

The town house was removed from the centre of George Street in 1814 And rebuilt on the west side, where its square tower and attractive circular spire can be seen, projecting beyond the roofs of the houses. Until local government reform in 1974, this continued to be the site of town council meetings and municipal government.

Even today, passing under the gatehouse, one has the sense of leaving one world and penetrating into another: in the days of pilgrimage, one was indeed passing into the sacred world of the monastery, with its own order, calendar and organisation. Archaeology has shown that **Bruce Street** respects the line of a road with a 1500 year old history and we know that **at least five monarchs of Scotland** came on pilgrimage by this route.

Facing Bruce Street, in fact, on the eastern side of George Street, is **King's Road**, which originally led from the landing place at the Isle of Whithorn across country to **St. Ninian's shrine.**

The award-winning Whithorn Story, (closed on my visit), told the story of the town of Whithorn's early Christian past, the churches on the site and the archaeology discovered there during the last century.

The Priory Gatehouse, Whithorn.

The Pend, Bruce Street.

The gatehouse preoccupied a central position in the mediaeval townscape of the burgh. It dominated the Burgh market place and the Royal Coat of Arms on its facade (the coat of arms of the Stuart kings) would have been a constant reminder to burgesses and pilgrims of the priory's status and of the source of its influence.

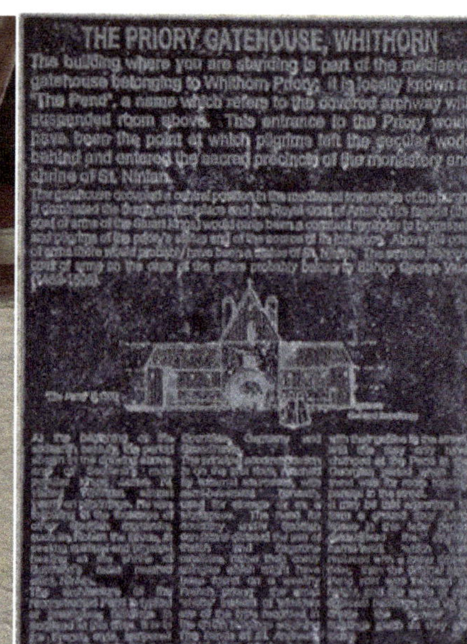

THE PRIORY GATEHOUSE, WHITHORN

The Plaque at the Priory Gatehouse reads:

The building where you are standing is part of the medieval gatehouse belonging to Whithom Priory; it is locally known as "The Pend", a name which refers to the covered archway with suspended room above.

This entrance to the Priory would have been the point at which pilgrims left the secular world behind and entered the sacred precincts of the monastery and shrine of St. Ninian

The gatehouse preoccupied a central position in the mediaeval townscape of the burgh. It dominated the Burgh market place and the Royal Coat of Arms on its facade (the coat of arms of the Stuart kings) would have been a constant reminder to burgesses and pilgrims of the priory's status and of the source of its influence. Above the coat of arms there would probably have been a statue of St Ninian. The smaller bishop's coat of arms on the cups of the pillars probably belong to Bishop George Vaus (1482-1508).

At the beginning of the sixteenth century, the period shown in the drawing above, one of Scotland's most popular Kings James IV visited Whithorn almost yearly on pilgrimage. He was following the footsteps of other Scottish monarch's such as Robert the Bruce in seeking spiritual and physical healing at the shrine of Scotland's most revered Saint, Ninian

The architecture of the reconstructed Pend is typical of prestigious buildings in Scotland at this time it is in the French style, tempered by Influences from the Low Counties, Germany and Scandinavia

The principal accommodation is on the first floor, reached by external staircases with semi-basement beneath, used for storage or as a workspace. The need for economy under Scottish conditions dictated the use of thatch and flagstone 'catslides', rather than costly shingle which might have been found on a wealthy French priory the small "shotts" instead of windows are of the type recorded in the 16th buildings adjoining the Pends at St Andrews

Other abbey pends also sit with their gables to the street and the may only have changed at the Pend in the Georgian period when the trend was for roofs running parallel to the street.

It may be that alterations to form a ground floor living space in this later period destabilised the original barrel vault which was replaced with a lower timber floor, then the original high Pend roof was reduced in height, and the walls of the adjacent buildings built up to create the terrace of buildings much as they are today.

The heraldic panel above, is likely to date from about 1500 and is one of only four Stuart coats of arms of this quality in Scotland. The Bishops' arms on the caps of the pillars are those of **Bishop Vaus** *(Vaux, Vans)*, who was bishop from **1482-1508.**

On the southernmost pillar, there are the arms of Bishop Vaus, surmounted by a crozier.

On the northern pillar, the arms of Bishop Vaus quartered with the arms of Shaw, (three closed cups argent on a ground azure), surmounted by a Bishop's mitre and mantled with a cope.

The focal point of Whithorn at the time when most of its houses were built would have been the tolbooth and gaol, now removed from the widest point of the street, at approximately the site of the War memorial. According to early travellers, there were also a series of "luckenbooths" for traders in the widest part of the street, which now provides extra parking spaces.

Weights and measures were also checked by the burgh, and burgh privileges to trade were jealously guarded; Wig town and Whithorn were frequently in dispute about dues payable and the destinations of profitable cargoes.

Without knowing the history of this part of the town, one might well agree with the eighteenth century minister, Christopher Nicholson, who commented that the town was "inconveniently narrow at both extremities and uselessly wide in the middle". The town house was removed from the centre of George Street in 1814 And rebuilt on the west side, where its square tower and attractive circular spire can be seen, projecting beyond the roofs of the houses. Until local government reform in 1974, this continued to be the site of town council meetings and municipal government.

George Street now designated an Outstanding Conservation Area, presents a mixture of relatively sophisticated town houses with single storey cottages in the vernacular Scottish tradition. Number 29 is a good example of a town residence, with circular-headed doorway, cornice and parapet with central panel. Others show by their steep roof pitches that they hark back to an earlier era, when they were thatched, and have small irregularly spaced windows, which seem to belong to the seventeenth century rather than the Georgian period.

The ¾ mile-long terrace of houses in George Street is almost complete, appearing just as it must have been developed in the early nineteenth century, with two exceptions: the Catholic Church, St. Martin's and St. Ninian's, was built on a gap site in the 1950's and the site at no. 61-3 George Street, which was burnt by fire in the 1930's, but rebuilt to the pre-existing building line.

By local tradition, the houses in Whithorn are generally painted in bright colours, with contrasting tones used for the walls and for the facings and courses, allowing textures and detailing to stand out, and for the buildings to be emphasised strongly, "coming forward" to the building line in cases where strong tones have been chosen.

Whithorn's chief historical treasure can only be glimpsed from George Street: the mediaeval Priory, archaeological site and Museum of Christian stones are hidden from view, and the early Christian (Fifth century) heart of Whithorn was probably sited on the gentle rise at the top of Bruce Street. The entrance to the Priory, however, constitutes one of Whithorn's most pleasing groups of buildings and provides a taste of the grandeur of what once lay behind it

Looking up Bruce Street towards Whithorn Priory from The Pend.

Framing the entrance to Bruce Street, "The Pend", a late mediaeval arch flanked by pillars with moulded caps and grandly surmounted by the Royal Arms of Scotland, tempts one off the main street towards the original site of St. Ninian's shrine A "Pend" in Scotland is used to refer to any passageway driven through a building, so creating a suspended room above it, but, notably, other monastic gateways in Scotland are also referred to as "Pends", such as that at St. Andrews.

The Pend building probably once stood much taller, and possibly had the form of a tower, familiar in monastery gateways elsewhere: the coat of arms on such an imposing building would have served as an advertisement of the power of Whithorn's Prior, who was under royal protection and had an all but regal power within his domain (known, in fact, as a "Regality").

Priory Museum and Bruce Cottage on Bruce Street.

Further up Bruce Street, facing the archaeological site is the museum, (The Whithorn Trust) containing one of the most important collection of carved and inscribed Christian stones in Scotland.

The stone forming the lintel to the door, which is dated 1730, was actually taken down from a small school building, which once stood nearly opposite the museum and which was excavated during the 1980's.

The stones were first gathered together from various sites by the Third Marquess of Bute, one of the great patrons of Christian archaeology, and the man who financed excavations at Whithorn in the last decade of the nineteenth century. The current appearance of the graveyard and crypts owes much to his reconstruction.

Priory Info board reads:

The Cradle of Christianity.

Whithorn Priory was home to one of Scotland's first Christian communities. Pilgrims came here to worship at the shrine of St Ninian - a mysterious figure widely credited with bringing Christianity to the region.

Key.

1. Knave:
A place of public worship. Pilgrims processed through it to St Ninian's shrine.

2. Cloister:
A walkway around a garden for reading and contemplation.

3. East end:
Where canons conducted daily services by the high altar.

4. St Ninian's Shrine:
The holiest part of the priory, beneath the high altar, where the saint's bones were kept.

5. Whithorn Parish Church:
Dedicated to St Ninian, the church was built here in 1822 on the site of the medieval priory.

FAITH IN STONE.

Scotland's oldest Christian monument, the Latinus Stone, was discovered here at the priory. It was carved in about AD 450.

You can see the stone and many other carvings in the museum next to the priory.

BUILDING WHITHORN.

In the 600s, a hilltop church stood separate from a shrine housing St Ninian's relics. The settlement was wealthy, possibly even royal. The residents feasted, and drank from brightly coloured vessels.

By the 800s, the faithful flocked to the shrine of St Ninian. The timber church and stone shrine lay at the heart of this holy landscape, while large halls housed pilgrims close by.

By 1500, the shrine had been absorbed into the body of the church. Local merchants traded along the route to the priory.

KEY DATES.

c. 431:
St Ninian is said to have died, and been buried here at Whithom. By the 700s a monastery has grown up around this shrine.

c.637:
The Venerable Bede is born. He goes on to promote St Ninian's fame in his writings.

c. 920:
Norsemen conquer Galloway. Shortly afterwards, skilled craftsmen begin to carve fine stone crosses here.

1497:
James IV makes the first of his many pilgrimages to Whithorn.

1890:
The 3rd Marquess of Bute funds excavations and restoration at Whithorn Priory

Priory info board reads:

"....Seeking forgiveness at Whithorn...

From 1296 until 1328, Scotland's war with England had brought the land to its knees and destroyed the health of its king - Robert the Bruce.
The ink on the Peace Treaty with England was barely dry before it became clear that Bruce was, indeed, a dying man.

At the age of 54, his body was wracked with a skin disease, possibly leprosy, after a lifetime of harsh living.

It is April 1329 and King Robert makes the final journey of his life.
Whatever his faults, the king is a pious man.
John Comyn's death by Bruce's hands at the High Altar in Dumfries, and the suffering of his loved ones, weighs heavily on his conscience.
After a long and uncomfortable journey he has arrived at Whithorn for one final pilgrimage and here, at St Ninian's Shrine, he prays for forgiveness.
On his return home, the king passes Glentrool, scene of his first victory over the English.

BRUCE AND THE CHURCH.

Once, it seemed that the whole world was against Robert Bruce - apparently a self-interested, sacrilegious murderer who stopped at nothing to gain the crown.
However, the Church of Scotland stood by him throughout his reign, an Independent Scotland freed the Church of interference from England.
Once peace was restored, King Robert worked with the Church to improve the wealth of the nation and the spiritual needs of its people

A DYING WISH

During his the Bruce had no time to atone for his sins.
He hoped one day to be free to Crusade in the Holy Land.
When that was no longer possible, his dying wish to Sir James Douglas was that his heart should be carried on Crusade.
On 7th June 1328, died peacefully and his heart was embalmed and placed in a casket.
A year later Douglas, his greatest friend, bore the casket into battle against the Moors in Spain but perished in the fight.
The heart, and the body of Douglas were brought home.
The cast of King Robert's skull on display in Dumfries Museum.
As well as war-damage, there is also bone missing from the upper jaw and nose and perhaps a sign that he did suffer from leprosy ?..."

Sign to St Ninian' Chapel in the Isle of Whithorn, (which is actually a peninsula).

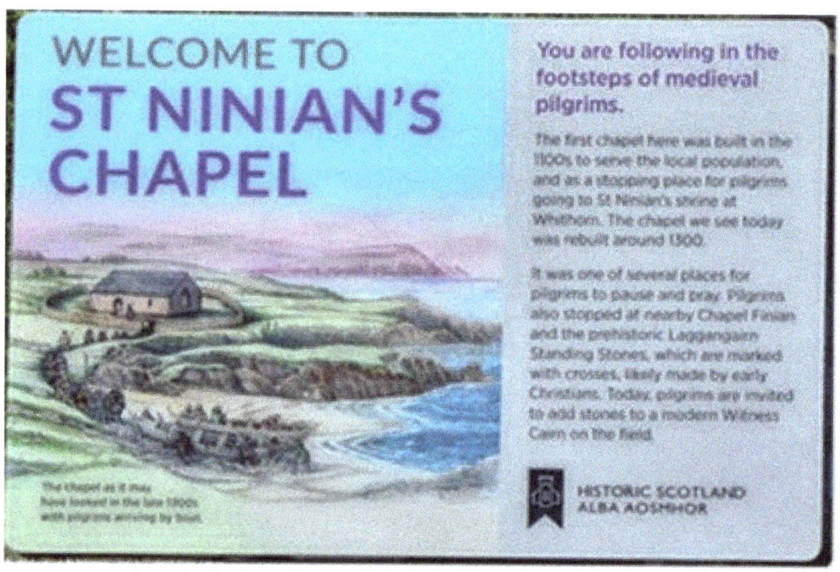

Info board at St Ninian's Chapel showing how the Chapel
may have looked in the late 1300s with pilgrims arriving by boat.

Info board reads:

"You are following in the footsteps of medieval pilgrims.
The first chapel here was built in the 1100s to serve the local population and as a stopping place for pilgrims going to see St Ninian's shrine at Whithorn (Priory).
The Chapel we see today was rebuilt around 1300.
It was one of several places for pilgrims to pause and pray.
Pilgrims also stopped at nearby Chapel Finian and the prehistoric Laggangairn Standing Stones, which are marked with crosses, likely made by early Christians.
Today pilgrims are invited to add stones to a modern Witness Cairn on the field."

Left: St Ninian's Chapel. Right: Picture courtesy of Duncan Thomson, Chairman, Strathleven Artizans.

Modern day pilgrims can add stones to a 'Witness Cairn' at the entrance to the field on which the chapel stands. Beside it is a bench commemorating the young fishermen from the Isle of Whithorn who died when their boat, the Solway Harvester, sank in 2000.
"...The Witness Cairn, Isle of Whithorn
This cairn was set up on the 11th May 1997 to celebrate St Ninian 397-1997 and provide the opportunity to add a stone to the cairn as a symbol of an act of witness which is completed or which is now pledged..."

Whithorn is a royal burgh in the Dumfries and Galloway region in the historic county of Wigtownshire in southwestern Scotland.
It lies on the peninsula between Luce and Wigtown bays and is one of the oldest Christian centres in Britain, founded about AD 397 by St. Ninian, who built a small whitewashed stone church—Whithorn, or "White House," from the Anglo-Saxon Huitaern—on the site of which a monastery was built about 1130.

St Ninian's shrine was one of the most famous places of pilgrimage in Scotland for centuries, and attracted visitors from the British Isles and beyond. In 1302, the future Edward II of England visited Whithorn while commanding an occupying army in Scotland. Scots apparently attempted to thwart him by removing a famous picture of the saint to Sweetheart Abbey - which then miraculously transported itself back to Whithorn

In 1329 Robert the Bruce endured a long, painful journey to Whithorn seeking a cure just three months before his death. The terminally-ill Robert's halting pilgrimage from his home in the **Parish of Cardross** to Whithorn early in that year may reflect the presence of that saint's relics at Bannockburn as well as Bruce's Carrick upbringing.

Equally, this final journey may have been penitential, echoing Robert's earlier grant to Whithorn Priory ***'because of the damage, injury and oppression of the church... by his past wars, and because of the devotion he has to St Ninian.'***

Bruce's son**, David II**, also visited Whithorn. At the **Battle of Neville's Cross in 1346**, two arrow-heads lodged in his face. Tradition has it that one of them resisted extraction until he visited the shrine. Accounts of the time state that after the battle, which the Scots had lost, David II was hiding under a bridge over the River Browney when his reflection was seen in the water by a group of English soldiers.

He was then taken prisoner by **John de Coupland**, who was leading the detachment and who had two teeth knocked out by the King. During the battle David II had been twice shot in the face with arrows. Surgeons attempted to remove the arrows but the tip of one remained lodged in his face, rendering him prone to headaches for decades.
James IV was a regular visitor to Whithorn, and Mary, Queen of Scots, made the last royal pilgrimage there in 1567.

The chapel was repaired and partly rebuilt in 1898 by the Marquess of Bute preserving its main features. The present ruins are rectangular, measuring internally 31' × 16' 6" (9.4 m × 5.0 m).

This building was probably erected to replace a 12th to early 13th century chapel, whose foundations were found during excavations and consisted of a nave, 17' 6" × 16' 6" (5.3 m × 5.0 m) with a square chancel.

The chapel stood within a contemporary enclosure wall, part of which is still standing - see foreground of pic. An outer enclosure may have once existed, (best seen in oblique sunlight), defining a roughly oval area 100' × 110' (30 m × 34 m). This outer enclosure may be of Celtic period.

There are no records of the chapel ever being used as a burial ground. St Ninian is chiefly remembered at Whithorn however, many places in Scotland are associated with his name, such as Saint Ninian's Isle in the River Garnock near Kilwinning. He converted the Southern Picts and therefore journeyed throughout many areas in southern Scotland.

12. Dunfermline Abbey – Final resting place for the King.

Bruce returned from his pilgrimage to Whithorn and died peacefully in his Manor House near the banks of the River Leven between Dumbarton and Renton dying on June 7, 1329, he was almost 55 years old.
The king's body was prepared for the journey to his final resting place in Dunfermline. His chest was opened and his heart and internal organs removed. Sir James Douglas was given his heart in an enamelled silver casket to be taken on a crusade against the Moorish invaders of southern Europe.

His breast bone and other internal organs were made ready to be buried in Saint Serfs Chapel located in present day Levengrove Park in Dumbarton. It was the custom for kings and queens to have two – sometimes three different burial places. Bruce's body was embalmed and made ready for the journey to Dunfermline to be buried beside his queen Elizabeth de Burgh who had died two years previously. After Bruce's body was prepared the embalmer would have taken part in a sacred ceremony; a bath in scented water and clothed in expensive robes, he would have been offered the best of food and wine and been given the hefty sum.

The distance to Dunfermline would have been about 60 miles. After leaving the manor house his body would pass through Saint Serf's Chapel, then to Old Kilpatrick and then Duntocher, then transported via Kirkintilloch to Dunipace where the entourage stopped for the night. The next day they would have made for Stirling crossing the field of Bannockburn, location of Bruce's greatest victory, and then to Cambuskenneth Abbey to spend the night. The next day the funeral cortege would travel through Kincardine and Culross before finally reaching Dunfermline.

The king would have been transported in a gilded hearse surmounted by a shield, a sword, and a royal crown. The hearse would have been pulled by plumed horses and everything decked in black and gold cloth. When making journeys across water the boats would have hoisted golden sails. Behind the king would have ridden his son, David II and his grandson the future Robert II fitted with expensive funeral garments, they would have ridden between his two greatest friends Sir Thomas Randolph and Sir James Douglas. Many other famous knights of Scotland would have been present wearing robes of mourning and decked in new shining armour paid for by the Scots Exchequer.

The King was carried through the towns and villages and past churches where people openly moaned and wailed when they witnessed the progress of their hero king's body to his final rest. The coffin itself would have had a painted wooden effigy of the king on top of it, known as a catafalque; again this was painted in black and gold. The Scots really excelled at this type of funeral heraldry, an upside down funeral crest would also have been carried at all times in front of the moving hearse as was customary at the time. On reaching Dunfermline Abbey he was laid under a chapel of gilded timber where great candles burned around the bier which was covered by a great gold cloth. It was said the light fell through the windows of the abbey upon the gorgeous garments of the abbot and the bishop.

The voices of these holy men rang clear and strong with comforting words as the chants of the congregation rose and fell as Robert the Bruce King of Scots was finally laid to rest in his most holy and revered tomb. The following year Sir James Douglas would find himself on the fields of Teba in southern Spain. He had joined forces with Alfonso and the Spanish army to fight back the Moorish army led by Osman. Douglas died while riding to the aid of his fellow Scots amidst the heat of battle. Legend states that he hurled the casket containing Bruce's heart into the Saracen's before he was cut down by many swords and spears. His body was boiled in vinegar and the bones returned to Scotland and buried at St Brides in Douglas. Bruce's heart was returned and sent to be interred in Melrose Abbey.

Left: Bruce Oak Axe Medallion. Right: Detail of Bruce's Tomb at Dunfermline Abbey.

Stained Glass Window. Dunfermline Abbey.
From left to right: Thomas Randolph, Earl of Moray, Sir James 'The Good' Douglas, King Robert I, James The Steward and Angus Og MacDonald of Islay.

Left: The Bruce Oak Heart returns to its original site in the Strathleven Estate in the Vale Of Leven, West Dunbartonshire.
Right: Sarah Crome's impression of the *'Manor of Cardross'* in the Dalquhurn area of the modern day village of Renton in the Vale Of Leven. Situated on the bank of the River Leven, Bruce's galley was rowed upstream to Loch Lomond and downstream to St Serf's Chapel at Dumbarton.

13."Bless the man in cloth of gold."

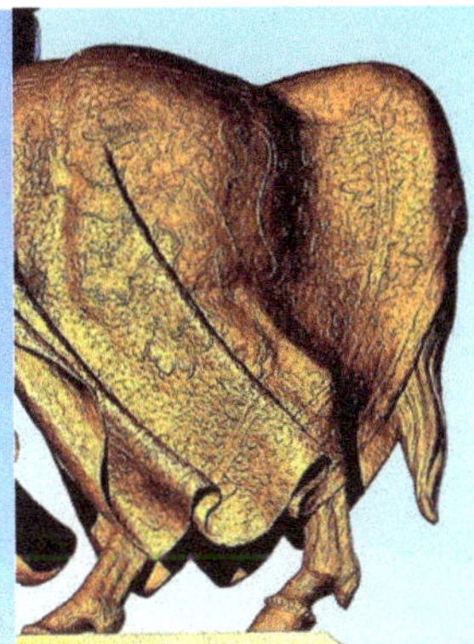

LIBERTY, by George Weir.

By the cross that Andrew bore,
By the sword that William wore,
By the crown our Robert swore,
We'll win our liberty.
Ca' the falcon frae the glen,
Ca' the eagle frae the ben,
ea' the lion frae his den,
Tae win our liberty.

By the man whose faith was old,
By the man they sold for gold,
By the man they'll never hold,
We'll win our liberty.
Ca' the thieves of Liddesdale,
Ca' the spears of Annandale,
Ca' the brave of Yarrow vale,
Tae win our liberty.

By the man who bends the bow,
By the man who plies the blow,
By the man who lays them low,
We'll win our liberty.
Ca' the banners frae the west,
Ca' the raven frae his nest,
Ca' the clans that dance the best
Tae win our liberty.

By the field that once was green,
By the shield of silver sheen,
By the swords in battle keen,
We'll win our liberty.
Bless the man whose faith we hold,
Bless the man in chains they sold,
Bless the man in cloth of gold,
We'll win our liberty.

This song was at the forefront of my mind when I took these pictures of the Bannockburn statue in Sept 2022.

14. A 21 Gun Royal Salute for the 750th Anniversary of the birth of King Robert I.

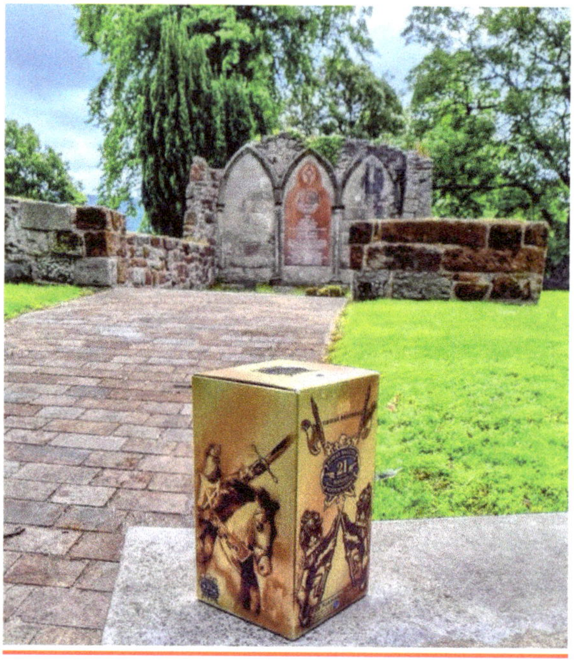

21 Year Old Chivas Regal Whisky at St Serf's Chapel, Levengrove Park, Dumbarton.

In celebration of Bruce's birthday. Bruce's viscera were interred here ahead of his body being taken to Dunfermline Abbey for burial.

Chivas Brothers Whisky Production site at Kilmalid is located in the Vale Of Leven and right by the Strathleven Estate where Robert the Bruce lived out the end of his life - and where he kept a pen for a lion. Before the entrance to the Chivas site there is the **Lions Gate Roundabout** named after two stone lion sculptures that have now been relocated to a private residence.

Bruce was said to have kept a pet lion somewhere in the vicinity of the modern day Lions Gate Roundabout. It is mentioned in the exchequer rolls that the lion was taken to Scone for Bruce's coronation.
Chivas Brothers has used Bruce iconography in their advertising and when their Paisley operation moved to Kilmalid they took their statue of Bruce with them to their new offices.

The Heart that has been featured in this story was carved from the salvaged Bruce Oak Tree that once stood near to here.

Chivas Brothers, their Bruce Statue, and The Lions Gate Roundabout.

Previously situated at their Paisley Offices – both Company and Statue now relocated to Kilmalid outside Dumbarton and near to the original site of the Bruce Oak in Strathleven.

A tempororay 'Lion Statue Monument' to Bruce at the Lions Gate Roundabout at the entrance to Chivas Bros site at Kilmalid.

15. In dedication - and with thanks.

This book is dedicated to the memory of James Bayne, Bonnybridge.

Supporter, Contributor & Friend to The King Robert the Bruce Heritage Centre, Renton.

With thanks to:

Duncan Thomson, Chairman, and Stephen Hughes of the Strathleven Artizans,
and all its members including:
Arthur Murdoch, Sgt At Arms and carver of the Bruce Oak Heart,
Simon Collings, the King's Special Envoy in Jerusalem.
and Cha Halliday for his Teba photographs.

And to **'Mrs G'** who accompanied me on this pilgrimage every step of the way -
and oor ain **Sma' Fowk** who have been brought up to understand the ground they walk on.
Finally, thanks to Paul Murdoch for his help forming the final book.

Jim Gilhooly, Vale of Leven.

Special thanks go to those who contributed to our Crowdfunding Campaign and those who placed an advanced order. Without your generosity, this book would not have been printed in the 750th year of King Robert the Bruce's birth. We thank you on his behalf.

Jamieson Aberdeen, Ev Brown, Richard Bruce, Rodney Bruce, Don Bruce, Robert and Rachel Bruce, Deb Bruce Gottlieb, Sherry Byrd, Colleen Casey, Iain Dowell, Stout Duncan, Bruce G, Calum Gilhooly, Sandy Gilhooly, Jim Gilhooly, Bob and Siobhan Gilhooly-Kimmerly, Cha and Mags Halliday, Steven Hughes, Neil Lochiel, David Lockhart, Kenny McAdam, Neal McNeilly, John Muir, Harry Peattie, Aimee Shields, Kate and Mike Smith, Duncan Thomson, Phyl Town Crier, Debra Lynne Walker, Alyson Wallace and three anonymous donations and three donations from our four-legged Artizans Molly, Oatly and Ayla.

www.ingramcontent.com/pod-product-compliance
Ingram Content Group UK Ltd.
Pitfield, Milton Keynes, MK11 3LW, UK
UKHW062000290726
14090UKWH00021B/1310

9 781036 907655